Gábor Naphegyi

Among the Arabs

A narrative of adventures in Algeria

Gábor Naphegyi

Among the Arabs
A narrative of adventures in Algeria

ISBN/EAN: 9783744793681

Printed in Europe, USA, Canada, Australia, Japan

Cover: Foto ©Andreas Hilbeck / pixelio.de

More available books at **www.hansebooks.com**

AMONG THE ARABS.

A NARRATIVE

OF

ADVENTURES IN ALGERIA.

BY

G. NAPHEGYI, M.D., A.M.,

AUTHOR OF "THE ALBUM OF LANGUAGE," "HISTORY OF HUNGARY," "LA CUEVA DEL DIABLO," ETC.

PHILADELPHIA:

J. B. LIPPINCOTT & CO.

1868.

AMONG THE ARABS.

WITH a ragged oiled-sailcloth valise, which contained but a single change of under-clothes, and they so ancient in appearance and so dilapidated in condition that they might have belonged to Methuselah, I stood on the deck of the schooner "Saint Martin," a small trading-vessel whose captain had been kind enough to give me a passage from Smyrna to Marseilles. The voyage was insufferably tedious: there was not a book in the vessel; and, to beguile the weary hours, I now and then volunteered to assist the cook, a good-natured, chatty old Frenchman, in the preparation of our meals. The captain, by his own account, was a proficient in the noble game of chess,—a delightful pastime on board ship; but to what purpose was his skill, when we had no chess-board? Being thus shut out from reading and chess-playing, I occupied myself, when not engaged in the duties of the *cuisine*, either in conversation with the captain or the crew, or in writing; and here again I found myself restricted, since paper was scarce and the voyage bade fair to be a long one, so that I had to be economical in expressing my thoughts, under the penalty of being deprived of this source of diversion.

On the 11th of September, 184–, we entered the
harbor of Marseilles, and, shouldering my not over-
heavy valise, I took leave of the captain, whom I now
looked upon as a friend, and with whom I promised to
correspond as soon as I had reached the "land of the
free," but who, I regret to confess, never cost me a
thought in after-years.

Eight silver *golden*, with the contents of the ragged
valise, constituted my entire worldly possessions; and
my friend the captain had exchanged the *golden* for
francs before I left the vessel. My money, used with
proper economy, would provide me with the means
of subsistence for several days: so I faced the future
with smiling countenance, and gave no thought to the
morrow.

It was my second visit to France, and, thinking
that France was not Austria, I gave myself very little
trouble about the want of a passport, considering myself too insignificant to be noticed even by a *gendarme*,
much less by the *Prefet Politique* of the port of Marseilles. But my fancied insignificance was of no avail
in this instance; for scarcely had I set foot on *terra
firma* when my passport was demanded, and, as I had
none, and confessed to being a political refugee from a
country that had just tried to overturn a monarchy,
I was politely refused a sojourn of more than twenty-
four hours on the soil of *La belle France*.

Whither to go I knew not, until my inventive genius
came to my assistance, and, almost mechanically, I bent
my steps to the quay where lay the staunch little
schooner "Saint Martin." Arrived there, I related my
sad story to my friend the captain, and he, being an
enthusiastic Jacobin, had pity on me, and offered me

the hospitalities of his vessel until he should sail again, promising to take me to a land which, if less glorious than France, certainly enjoyed more freedom. Being able to do no better, I resigned myself to my fate and accepted his kind offer, to the great delight of the crew of the vessel, who had become sincerely attached to me during the voyage from Smyrna; and the consciousness of this feeling on their part served materially to alleviate the bitterness of my disappointment.

After I was fairly reinstated in my old abode, the question naturally arose, "Whither am I to be carried next?" for in reality I was no longer the master of my own actions, and had to abide the chance which might charter the vessel for this or that part of the world. Yet, after all, of what consequence was it to me where I might be taken? I was an exile from my native land, and it mattered not to what part of the globe fortune should turn my steps.

The seven francs with which I had gone ashore, the sum total of my worldly wealth, had already dwindled to five; and I resolved not to allow my necessities to press too heavily on the remainder, since I was determined that, whatever the country which my destiny might design as a permanent or a transient home, I would not enter it entirely devoid of means. So, taking one franc more, to buy a fresh supply of paper, pens, and ink, I sewed up the remaining four in the pocket which would have contained my watch had I possessed that useful piece of mechanism.

Twelve days passed away in suspense and anxiety, lying idly in the harbor of Marseilles: on the thirteenth the captain brought the cheering news that he had chartered his vessel for Algiers. Africa, then, was my

new destination, and I must confess that I was by no
means indifferent to this announcement; for, being
young and of an adventurous disposition, with an ardent
love of travel, the prospect of visiting a country which
I had never yet seen could not be otherwise than
pleasing,—though I would have still more rejoiced had
we been destined to America. I had visited the far
East, had rambled through Egypt, was familiar with
the remotest corners of Europe; but Algeria was *terra
incognita.*

The schooner took in its cargo, and eight days after
the charter had been signed we weighed anchor and
steered for Algiers. Our ship's company was the same
as on the preceding voyage, with the exception of the
second mate; and our passenger list had been augmented by two individuals, one of whom was part-
owner of the cargo. He was a native of Algiers, of
the Jewish faith, not yet thirty years of age, and was
one of the richest merchants in the place of our destination. Once a year he made a trip to France to attend
to his purchases. On this occasion he was accompanied
by his bookkeeper, a German, and with whom I easily
became acquainted; so that the voyage bade fair to be
a pleasant one to me. Oser ben Levi, the Algerine
merchant, after our first day at sea, manifested a friendly
interest in my desire to learn the Arabic language;
and, though he was able to make himself only half
understood in French, yet with the help of the bookkeeper, with whom I could freely converse in German,
he managed to become my instructor, the bookkeeper
also aiding in the task. Nor were they disappointed in
the results of their kind offices; for—I believe I may
say it without vanity—I made an apt scholar.

When in the course of conversation they became aware of the condition of my finances, Oser ben Levi proffered me the hospitalities of his house, which I gladly accepted; and, although it is not likely that these pages will ever meet his eye, I cannot refrain from the expression of my heartfelt gratitude for the many kindnesses and manifestations of friendship which, during my stay in Algiers, I received under his hospitable roof.

Algiers,—or, as it is called in the original, Al-Jezira, —the capital of Algeria, is situated northwesterly of a bay of the same name on the Mediterranean. It lies on the northern slope of a mountain called Banjarin, which rises some six hundred feet above the level of the bay; and the city itself, like most other Arabic or Moorish cities of large dimensions, forms an amphitheatre, terminating in an esplanade, on which stands, in this instance, the old citadel, or *Kasbah*. It is supposed that this citadel, as well as the harbor, was built by Barbarossa in 1530; but there exists considerable doubt respecting the real founder of the Kasbah.

The appearance of Algiers is grand and imposing: especially must it seem so to the European who has never been in the East nor seen any of the cities of Spain. But this impression passes away as soon as the traveller reaches the interior of the city, which compares very unfavorably with the imposing aspect of the exterior. The streets are narrow and inconvenient; the houses are built of stone or brick, and, with a few exceptions, are whitewashed, this operation being performed annually; while the height of the buildings seldom reaches more than one story over the basement, and the roofs are flat, like those of the houses in South

America. Each roof is furnished with one or more water-tanks, placed there to receive the rain, and resembling huge, broad chimney-stacks.

Upon my arrival at Algiers, I was placed in charge of the German, with orders from his employer to conduct me to his abode and bring me the next day to his store or office, which was situated in one of the principal thoroughfares of the city.

Although comfortably installed in my new home on Arabian soil, and with every thing around me calculated to engage my attention by its utter novelty, I could not resist a feeling of sadness as I thought of the distance that separated me from kindred and home; and anxiety for the future served to intensify my depression of spirits.

The next day I was taken to the office of Oser ben Levi, where I was presented to his father, a man of threescore and ten, of most venerable aspect, with a snow-white beard covering the whole breadth and length of his chest. I greeted him with the salaam of the East, but could not, with all my practice in the Arabic language on board the vessel, understand one of the sentences which he addressed to me, which, however, were translated for me by the son into half French, and by the bookkeeper into German. Eli ben Chaim was the head of the concern, carrying on trade mostly with France, Tunis, and Morocco. He had, during a long career of successful enterprise, accumulated a large fortune, and was considered one of the wealthiest merchants of Algiers.

The foreign population of Algiers consists principally of French; the natives comprise Arabs, Turks, Moors, Koloughs, and Jews. During the hours of business all seem to belong to the same class; but as soon as the business hours have passed, each man betakes himself to his own class and kindred. Passing through the streets in the evening, especially in that part of the city which is not central, you can have no difficulty in knowing the quarter to which each person whom you meet belongs. Nowhere is this distinction more strongly marked than in the quarter inhabited by the Jews: here they live, pray, and enjoy themselves, and are very rarely disturbed by the intrusion of one who does not belong to their creed.

When, after the business hours, we approached the house of Eli ben Chaim, I could see no difference between it and the houses of his neighbors;—all presented nearly the same outside appearance. Knocking on the door by means of a brass handle attached to it, a young Israelite of the menial class soon answered the summons, and I was at once ushered into a wide, commodious hall, the walls and ceiling of which were perfectly white, while the tiled floor was of a blood-red color, and had apparently been painted but a short time before. Chairs and benches, made of the wood of the locust-tree, were ranged against the wall, and in the centre stood a table of the same material, covered with a faded green cloth.

Silence reigned throughout the house, as though the merchant, his son, and the servant were its only occupants. Beseeching me to make myself thoroughly at home, my friends asked to be excused for a short time, and left me alone. Not long afterwards, Oser ben Levi again made his appearance,—this time, however, not dressed in the European fashion, but his tall figure draped in a black taffetas robe that reached from his neck

to his ankles. Making the Arabic salutation by crossing his hands over his breast, and bowing profoundly,
he signed to me to follow him, saying that he would,
by his father's permission, present me to the family.
I followed him mechanically through a long corridor
which appeared to extend through the depth of the
house, and lighted by two oil lamps suspended from
the ceiling. At the end of this corridor a large folding
door stood open: here he made me a sign to enter first;
for, as I afterwards had occasion to observe, the Arab
will never enter a room, nor be seated after entering,
before his guest.

Passing through the folding door, I beheld a scene
which made an impression on my mind that can never
be effaced. The atmosphere that I breathed here was
so different from that of the outer world, the scene before me was so utterly unexpected, that I stood spell-
bound, unable to advance a single step; and I know
not how long I should have remained rooted to the
spot, had not my friend gently taken me by the arm
and led me forward. At the farther end of the room,
in a high and large arm-chair covered with the costliest material, sat the venerable head of the family.
His dress consisted of a heavy silk robe, of a yellowish
tint, which hung in ample folds about his stately figure;
his feet were encased in embroidered sandals; while on
his head was a rich white turban, his long silvery locks
mingling with the snow-white beard that covered his
breast. He looked like the high-priest so well depicted by the disciple of Murillo, Baltazar Chavez, in
the well-known painting of the marriage of the Virgin
and St. Joseph, seen at the Louvre in Paris. Near him,
partly reclining, partly leaning on his chair, were his

three daughters, the oldest of whom was not more than twenty-two years of age, yet was already the mother of two children; while the other two had seen, respectively, only eighteen and sixteen summers. They were dressed in that Eastern style that becomes women so well. On their heads were light turbans of gay colors, adorned with pearls and precious stones; while their dresses were of that material which is brought by caravans from the far East, and which is worn only by those whose means enable them to pay a high price. Their raven-black hair, falling in heavy curls over their partially-bared shoulders, enshrined their faces, the beauty of whose complexion was enhanced by the light tinge of brown that denotes the origin and nationality of their creed.

Although the Jew, all over the world, has preserved the type of his nationality by never marrying out of his creed, each country has made its own distinctive impression upon his features; and especially is this the case with the females. Compare the Jewess of Russia with the Jewess of Italy or of Spain: you will at once know that both are of the seed of Jacob, but in the one you will see the Northern phlegm and dispassionateness, in the other the fire and animation of the Southern clime; and the farther south you travel, the more noticeable becomes this difference.

Not far from the venerable patriarch, on a divan of the richest cushions, sat the wife of my friend the young merchant, her two children playing at her side and forming a very interesting picture. She was a Portuguese lady, the daughter of a rich banker of Lisbon.

My young friend, in introducing me to the family,

used the French language; and heartily glad was I to find that I should be enabled to express my sentiments in a language understood by all present. So well, indeed, did the ladies converse in French that, but for the Asiatic character of their dress and the novel embellishments of the apartment, I might have imagined myself in a saloon of the Faubourg St. Germain. I afterwards found that their proficiency in the language was not to be wondered at, since they had resided in Paris for about six years and had received their education there. Their mother had been dead for several years, and at her death the superintendence of the household devolved upon the eldest daughter, who, as I have already stated, was now married, her husband being a rich jeweller, trading mostly with Portugal and Spain, but who at present was absent from home.

They had all been made aware of my circumstances by their brother; and in the course of conversation during this my first visit, I was repeatedly invited to settle in Algiers and devote myself to the practice of my profession. I freely confess that had my fair friends promised to become my patients, the temptation to accept would have been almost irresistible.

After a prolonged stay,—too long, indeed, for etiquette,—I took my leave, receiving from the father an urgent invitation to call every evening except that of the Sabbath day, which is most rigorously observed by the Algerine Jews. No visitors are received at any time except some male member of the family be present; and, as the business of my friends closed at five o'clock in the afternoon, that was the hour that opened to me the doors of a house which I visited nearly every day during my short stay in Algiers.

Attached to the medical staff of the garrison at Algiers was a Dr. H——, from Strasbourg,—a gentleman of German parentage, and the first physician who had entered Algeria with the troops after its conquest by France. He had travelled extensively throughout the whole French colony, and had even ventured beyond the military lines into the region occupied by the Kabyls, the deadliest foes of the invaders. I had formed his acquaintance through the good offices of my friend the German bookkeeper of Oser ben Levi; and it afforded me a great deal of pleasure, not only on account of his personal merits, but as giving me the opportunity of intercourse with the prominent scientific men of the place. I also profited greatly by several visits which I made in his company to the military hospitals of the French garrison.

In the course of our frequent rambles through the city, he pictured to me, in glowing colors, his numerous travelling adventures among the natives, which so excited my curiosity that I determined to visit the interior and see for myself. The dangers of the journey did not deter me: I had nothing to lose but life, and I was so completely cut off from all that makes life dear that I cared not what risks I incurred: I made up my mind, therefore, to start on the journey at the first opportunity. Nor did I have long to wait. An expedition was soon to set out from Tlemcen to establish a military post in one of the oases, some seventy miles in the Sahara; and I resolved to accompany it, if possible.

There is very little to be said of the Algiers of to-day; for it is rapidly losing its Moorish characteristics and becoming a French city. The better class of the

native population are adopting French habits and manners; while the lower class, through constant intercourse with their conquerors, are losing the attractive-
ness which they would have to a stranger were their -
customs and manner of living the same as those of
their ancestors.

Above the town are numerous fountains, by which it
is plentifully supplied with water, conveyed into the
city by means of aqueducts and reservoirs. There are
ten mosques, which, however, had no attractions for
me, since he who has seen the St. Sophia of Constantinople has seen all the mosques of Mohammedanism.
The Cathedral is of recent date, and is not by any
means an architectural masterpiece; while the four
courts of justice deserve no particular notice here.
The bazaars and shops are numerous, and are attractive
on account of the variety and beauty of the wares sold
in them.

Among the various classes of professional men, the
bankers occupy the foremost rank; for there are at
least three hundred in the city, although its entire
population does not exceed one hundred thousand.
Besides the large dealers or wholesale merchants, there
are innumerable money-changers, ship-brokers, inter-
preters, &c.; and during business hours the bustle of
the merchants' quarter might serve to remind one in no
slight degree of the activity and hurry of Wall Street
in New York.

Steamers ply regularly between Algiers, Bona, Oran,
Bougiah, and Philippeville; but this is entirely the result of French enterprise, as the trade carried on by
the natives is of very little consequence. The Jewish
portion of the population is, almost without exception,

actively engaged in the retail trade; the natives manufacture some silk and woollen fabrics, trinkets indicative of no great amount of taste, saddlery of the roughest description, and a few other insignificant articles.

The smaller bazaars, and especially those in which Algerine productions are offered for sale, are owned principally by Jews and natives, and are very similar to the bazaars of the lower order in Constantinople. The unfortunate individual who enters one of these is very glad to get out again; for, if he appears at all verdant, he is pulled and hauled from one side to the other, until at last he makes a purchase, although on entering he may not have had the slightest intention to do so, merely in order to get rid of the importunities of the noisy dealer.

Ordinarily, the price of living in Algiers is very low: for one hundred and fifty francs, or about thirty dollars, a month, one can live with comfort in any of the second-class hotels.

The harbor and the citadel, or Kasbah, are the only truly monumental works of Algiers. The former was built by Barbarossa in 1530,—its mole or pier being about five hundred and eighty feet long and one hundred and forty wide, and extending from the mainland to an islet, on which is another castle, or fort, provided with batteries as a means of defence against an enemy approaching by way of the sea.

During my stay I visited the principal temples of worship at the time of service,—the mosque of the Arab on Friday, the synagogue of the Jew on Saturday, the cathedral of the Christian on Sunday,—not as an indifferent spectator, but deeply impressed by the rites and ceremonies of each.

2*

Provided with letters of introduction from my friend Dr. H—— and from the General Intendant of the French army in Algiers to Viscount L——, of Tlemcen, brevet-general to head the expedition, I bade adieu to the generous friends and acquaintances whom I had made during my short stay in Algiers. At the moment of leave-taking, I received, from the kind-hearted Oser ben Levi, a letter, which, as I afterwards found, provided me with sufficient means to enable me to travel independently, and was, besides, a recommendation to his correspondents at the various places through which I was to pass, to extend to me any assistance that I might need. Noble friend! his heart was a treasury of the virtues commended by Moses, by Mohammed, and by Christ, and yet he dressed in that religious garb called the Jewish.

Before setting out for Tlemcen, however, I determined to visit the eastern part of Algeria, to take advantage of the opportunity, which might never again present itself, of examining the ruins in the neighborhood of Constantina, a town built on the site of the Cirta of the ancients, the capital of the Numidian kings.

The situation of Constantina gives it an imposing appearance. It stands on a rocky peninsula, seventeen hundred feet high, formed by the course of the Rummel, and is about one hundred and eighty miles from Algiers and forty from the Mediterranean. It is surrounded by a wall which, judging from the elegance of its structure and the sculptured decorations over the four gates of entrance, was built by the Romans. This wall is the only piece of architecture in Constantina which is worthy of admiration. As in all other Eastern cities, the streets are very narrow, and laid out without the slightest regard to the rules of symmetry; but the houses have slanting roofs, which gives them considerable of a European aspect. The principal business is the trade in corn, carried on with Tunis, and in the products of Central Africa, with the tribes to the south. The environs of the city strongly remind one of the south of Italy : the fields are beautifully laid out and thoroughly cultivated.

The morning after my arrival I spent in rambling among the ruins that abound in and around the city. Anciently all the roads in Numidia converged towards Cirta, which, judging from the extent of its ruins, must have spread over a much larger area than the present town. These ruins are all of Roman architecture. The town was ravaged in the year 311, but was afterwards rebuilt by Constantine, whose name it took. The present population is about thirty thousand : of these not more than three thousand are Europeans ; the remainder are Arabs, Turks, Jews, and a few subjugated Kabyls.

From Constantina I proceeded to Bona, eighty-five miles to the northeast, my curiosity having been excited by the glowing description given me by my friend Dr. H——, of the ruins of Hippo-Regius, once the see of St. Augustine, but destroyed by the Caliph Othman. I was doomed to disappointment, however ; for when on the spot they failed to awaken any of the enthusiasm with which I had looked forward to beholding them.

They are about a mile distant from Bona. That they were magnificent in their proportions at one time is beyond doubt, but at present they are little better than rubbish-heaps, lacking even the interest which sometimes attaches to ruins that have some tradition,

real or imaginary, connected with them by the inhabitants of the vicinity. Few of the townspeople of
Bona knew any thing of their history; but I acci-
dentally became acquainted with a French priest, who,
like myself, was interested in visiting the ruins, and
who related to me some historical facts, which, however, had more bearing upon the life and actions of St.
Augustine than upon those of the ancient kings.
Among the ruins are some halls on which the cor-
roding hand of Time has been laid but lightly. They
are very spacious, and the doors by which they are
reached are supported by two pillars with superbly-
sculptured capitals. There are also two huge animals
cut out of stone; but whether they were intended to
represent lions or the sphynx I was unable to determine.

An Arab shepherd, who was grazing his flock close
by, told us of a place near to—or rather under—the
ruins, which was the spot set apart for the reception of
the deceased Numidian kings, and offered to conduct
us thither for fifty sous. The price was paid at once,
and willingly, for we were both in quest of historical
reminiscences,—the priest for those which concerned
his patron saint, and I for any thing relating to the
Numidian monarchs.

Struggling over rough heaps of stone, from the
crevices of which some hideous lizard every moment
emerged, we reached at last an opening scarcely large
enough for the admission of one person at a time. This
opening led to a subterranean passage, which we had
to traverse in the dark, our only guide being the stick
of the Arab, to which we clung tightly, for fear of becoming separated or of stumbling over some rubbish.

I felt the chilly dampness creeping through my frame; and the echo of our footsteps resounded gloomily from the unseen walls. After proceeding in silence for about five minutes, my companion addressed me in Latin, not daring to use the French, lest the guide should understand our conversation. He expressed deep regret at the hasty thoughtlessness with which we had trusted ourselves to the guidance of a man whom we had never seen before, and who, above all, was a Kabyl. What evil genius could have possessed us, to cause us to venture on so hairbrained an undertaking? Might we not be suddenly attacked by our Arab guide, and pay with our lives the penalty of our unaccountable rashness? Might he not have decoyed us into this living tomb with the design of robbing us? And so many were the conjectures of my priestly friend that at last I, who till then had not so much as dreamed of danger, began to experience a most uncomfortable sense of fear and anxiety and to wish myself well out of the whole affair; but, reflecting that there was now no remedy, and that the wise thought had not come till the foolish step had been taken, I summoned up my wavering courage and resolved to face unshrinkingly whatever danger might be in store for us.

It was ten o'clock in the morning when we entered the ruin: the day was beautifully clear, and the sun shining brightly; but in that subterranean passage it was night,—ay, darker than the darkest night, a darkness that might be felt. I could not help feeling considerable uneasiness, in spite of my resolution to face the worst; for the Kabyls are a treacherous race, and the deadliest foes the French have on the soil of

Algeria, and, although I was no Frenchman, I knew very well that our guide, if his intentions were evil, would trouble himself very little indeed about my nationality. In the midst of these reflections, the Arab, without a word of warning, released his hold of the stick by which he had been leading us, and we could hear his footsteps grow faint and fainter as he rapidly retreated from where we stood.

Here, then, we were, almost paralyzed by fear and astonishment, unable even to utter a cry, and filled with anxiety as to what the next moment might bring forth; for it seemed as if the gloomy forebodings of my companion were indeed about to be realized. Danger, when we know from what quarter it approaches, can be met with unmoved countenance, and a courageous determination to combat it; but when we are conscious of its presence, and at the same time know not whence it comes nor how to avoid it, it assumes a far more terrible aspect.

Thus it was with us: wrapped in the profoundest darkness, and not knowing at what minute the blade of an assassin might be plunged into our heart, no wonder that we were horror-struck, and could neither move nor speak for some minutes.

At last, however, collecting my senses, I shouted after the retreating Arab, calling him by all the names I could invent in the Arabic tongue; but the only answer I received was the echo of my voice, repeated more frequently than I cared to hear it; for these very repetitions served to remind me of the danger, and impressed me with the conviction that there were more passages than one,—so that, even if assassination were not to be our doom, we might be utterly powerless to extricate ourselves from the trap we had so foolishly entered. While these thoughts were passing through my mind, my companion, trembling from head to foot, was muttering his prayers and commending our souls to God.

Throughout my life, I have never allowed misfortune to gain the mastery over my feelings longer than the time necessary to measure its full extent; and, once acquainted with that, I set about finding the means of extricating myself. Recovering from my momentary stupefaction, I grasped the hand of my companion, who still continued his prayers, and dragged him along with me, to endeavor, if possible, to make our way to the entrance; but hardly had we taken twenty steps in what I supposed to be a backward direction, when our heads came in contact with something that appeared to be above us. Whether it was in consequence of the blow, or arose from my peculiar state of mind, I know not; but so it was that I could not comprehend how it happened that while with the guide we had encountered no obstacles, now we could hardly take a single step backwards without coming in contact with some projection.

"Courage, Monsieur l'Abbé," I said to my companion in misfortune, at the same time standing sorely in need of some one to encourage myself. However, I did not yield to despair, as he did; but I was perplexed, and knew not what to suggest. After a few moments I proposed that the priest should remain where he was, while I proceeded to explore; but this he would not hear of, since, as he said, if I should miss a step we would be separated, and deprived of the power of mutual consolation, which would make our position even worse than it was at present. I then bethought me of another expedient. I took my neck-tie and every thing else available to make a cord as a guide, and this, with the material provided by my companion, formed one that would answer my purpose tolerably well. The cord made, he took one end and I the other. He remained stationary, while I advanced, and when I could proceed no farther I halted and he advanced towards me, keeping the cord stretched tight. Backward, as we thought, we went, until it seemed as if we had surely gone ten times the distance we had travelled when entering, and still there was not the faintest glimmer of light, not the slightest prospect of finding our way out of the labyrinth. I groped around, to ascertain if we were near any wall; but I could find none: the place seemed to be a vast chaos.

At last, fatigued and despondent, we sat down to rest and gather strength for a new exploration. I felt the difficulties of our position more keenly than I can express. "What," said I to my friend, "if our exertions should prove as fruitless as those we have already made? What will be the result, what our fate?" "Death by starvation," answered the shivering priest, in a hollow, sepulchral voice; and "Death!" repeated the echo tenfold throughout the cave. We were even deprived of the poor consolation of speaking to each other; for the mockery of the echo was intolerable, and made our situation seem worse than in reality it was.

After a new and unsuccessful trial, I discovered that I had a few matches, with which I was always provided to light my cigars. I proposed to ignite one of them, so as to have at least a clearer although momentary conception of what seemed destined to be our living grave. My companion was overjoyed at the discovery, and was almost ready to believe our troubles were at an end. The match was lighted, and by its dim, momentary blaze we beheld what to us was a fearful sight. We stood in the centre of a large space, which, to our heated imagination, seemed to be miles in circumference; and—oh, horror!—not more than ten paces from us we beheld a body of water, which to our over-strained vision appeared to be an immense lake. "I shall not move one step farther," ejaculated my companion; and, sitting down on the ground, he grasped my knee, so as not to lose hold of me. "Nor I," was my reply; and, taking a seat beside him, I made myself as comfortable as was possible under the circumstances. I made up my mind to resign myself to my fate, and let it take its course, since I had not the power to combat it. I took a cigar out of my pocket, lighted it, and sought consolation in puffing away at the weed, which had never been so welcome as at that moment. The poor priest could not enjoy that consolation, for he did not use tobacco; but instead, either from fear or exhaustion, he soon fell into an uneasy sleep.

I had five matches remaining; and I ventured to indulge in the extravagance of lighting one more, to see at least what time of day it was. The hands pointed to two. We had, therefore, been in this dismal place for four hours, which seemed to me like so many years. I continued to seek consolation in puffing at my cigar, until my mind originated a brilliant idea.

When I met the priest before we entered, I noticed that he had a large book under his arm. That book, thought I, will be our salvation; and, trembling with eagerness, I commenced to put my plan into execution. Leaning over my sleeping companion and groping around in the dark, I found the book at his side; and, oh, how happy was I to feel its size and volume! for on the number of its leaves depended more or less our hope of rescue. Without further ado, I set myself to work, and one by one I tore the leaves from the book. I then twisted each leaf into a long, thin roll; and, this done, I found, upon counting them, that there were nearly four hundred. Now commenced my arithmetical calculation. Each of those paper torches, when lighted and used economically, will last about thirty seconds; two will thus be consumed in a minute, and one hundred and twenty in an hour; four hundred will last, then, almost three hours and a half; and in that time surely some outlet will be found. I was so happy at the prospect of deliverance, and so proud of what I considered an ingenious invention, that I could not refrain from waking up the priest and communicating to him the scheme by which I intended to find the way out. He, bewildered from the effect of his dream and inspired by the hope of being rescued from what he called a living grave, clasped my knee in wild frenzy, but in a moment he released it; for just then it occurred to him that I had, by my ingenious invention, destroyed the work on which he had been occupied for years. The book, it appeared, was a collection of notes, gathered by himself, on the life of St. Augustine, whose biography, which he had almost completed, he had intended to publish on his return to France.

I could appreciate his sadness and grief, and tried to

console him, offering him the alternative of writing the biography of his patron saint over again, or dying of starvation in the cave. After some reasoning, he admitted that I was in the right, and added, with the fervor of a true believer, "May the life of the saint whose biography will be the light to shine before us, lead us from this darkness to the bright light of day!"

The priest reasoned well; but his reasoning was based on faith, and on faith alone. He even attributed my happy idea to the inspiration of his patron saint; for if he had not been writing the history of the saint he would not have had the book with him, and I would have had no supply for torches; therefore it was the saint who should lead us out of the darkness, and not the mere material on which the saint's life was recorded. My reasoning was different. I attributed the idea to the force of circumstances, while I viewed the paper simply as a combustible, and would have greatly preferred some newspapers or other material which would have served my purpose better. If the saint had any thing to do with the matter, the inspiration of precaution would have been more opportune had it come before we entered.

Be that as it might, the experiment was at least worth trying, and I at once prepared to put it into execution. In the first place, I carefully thought out the measures to be taken; and I believe that Wellington, on the eve of Waterloo, did not proceed with greater caution than I did at this critical moment; for it was our last hope, and I would not for a moment entertain the idea of failure.

Giving the priest a quantity of these rolls, and a match, I ignited one myself and lighted roll number one; cautiously I advanced, bidding my companion remain where he then was, and only to light one when I should advise him that I had lost the direction of his position. I was not wrong in my calculation: each roll lasted about thirty seconds; and, as far as I could see by their dim light, I was sure we were in an immense subterranean cave. Farther and farther I had advanced from the priest, but as yet I could see no outlet, and my heart commenced to sink within me. Still, I did not despair, but went in another direction. All I desired was to get to the wall or side of the cave; that once found, I would economize my torches and guide myself by feeling only. But all my efforts had thus far been fruitless; and I resolved to call the priest to my side and hold a council of war. I called out to him, and, guided by the light in my hand, he bent his steps towards the spot where I stood, and reached it in safety.

It was now four o'clock, and the anxiety which tormented me brought forth great drops of perspiration to my brow. The disappointment contributed not a little to my sadness, for I had been so sure of success, and I feared now that our last hope was gone. To my friend I dared not confide my misgivings; for, as his book had by this time been half burned up, my fears would only have caused him to feel the misery of our situation more keenly.

To make matters worse, I now felt thirsty, my tongue was parched, and—reluctant though I might be to admit it—I was becoming feverish. And what wonder it should be so? Had I not for six hours been exposed to the worst mental torment imaginable, each minute augmenting the torture?

With the fever that I felt creeping through my veins, came another torment, its natural result. I saw in my overheated imagination the niches of the tombs of the Numidian kings; I saw the heavy stone covers rise from the sarcophagi, and the former masters of the realm came forth, attired in their rich, fantastic armor. Nearer and nearer, with solemn step, those stately figures approached, till I could hear the rattling of their swords and feel their ice-cold breath. Steadily onward they came, as though about to visit retribution on the rash intruders upon the privacy of their sepulchres,—until sight failed me, all became blank, and I sank exhausted to the earth.

The cool dampness of the ground had a beneficial effect, in alleviating the fever which was burning within me; and the visions of my transient delirium passed away, to return no more. It was now the priest's turn to assume the office of consoler; and when I reproached him with the utter absence of assistance from his patron saint, he assured me that I was the cause, since I had no faith. "Ah," thought I, "I will believe implicitly in saints of much lower degree than St. Augustine, if they will but save us from the death by starvation which now threatens us;" and I tried to convince my companion that the meanest infidel, the most insignificant Arab, could do more to extricate us from this labyrinth than the entire community of saints.

As we were thus conversing, a marvellous change ᴏok place. Our position assumed a widely different aspect. At first I thought it was only another chimera ᴊf a disordered imagination; but no: this time my eyes were wide open, I was not delirious, I was in full

3*

possession of my senses. And yet what I saw appeared too supernatural, too grand, to be any thing but a vision; for in an instant a many-colored light filled the cave, penetrating to its remotest corners and giving to it an aspect almost unearthly. At that moment I was too much occupied with the idea of rescue from the horrible place which I had almost begun to think was to be my grave, to remember any thing of Dante and his description of the infernal regions; but often since then has it seemed to me that the Italian poet must surely have witnessed something of the kind before his imagination could have been so vividly inspired.

Quick as thought I was on my feet, and, grasping the hand of my friend, I exclaimed, "We are saved!" He, bewildered by the strange spectacle, at once bethought him of his patron saint, and attributed the sudden illumination to a supernatural power; I, on the contrary, remembering to have witnessed just such a phenomenon while on a visit to the world-renowned salt-mines of Wieliczka in Poland, was not long in coming to the conclusion that the light proceeded from pyrotechnic fires kindled by human hands.

We could now see the cave in its true dimensions, which were very far from coinciding with those our excited imaginations had given to it. The place of exit was not ten paces from where we stood; and we could explain the apparently vast size of the cave in the darkness by no other hypothesis than that we had travelled in a circle, and had, in our anxiety and uncertainty, mistaken a molehill for a mountain. We ran at once towards the outlet, but, before we had reached it, were met by our Arab, whom we had so wrongfully suspected of sinister motives, carrying lighted torches, and full of apology for his long delay in reappearing. Rather long indeed, thought I; for those six hours had seemed as many months; but now we were saved, and the remembrances of fever, fatigue, excitement, sepulchres, Numidian kings, and patron saints, all passed away at the thought that we were about to see once more the blessed light of day. The Arab wished to explain, but I was in no listening mood : hurriedly I urged him forward until we arrived at the surface, when, feeling as though I had been rescued from the grave, I hastened to the nearest hut, to procure some refreshment after my disagreeable adventure.

My companion did not follow immediately, but entered into conversation with the Arab; and when I was nearly ready to set out on my return to Bona, he made his appearance, bearing the remainder of his history, while he had sent the guide to look for any stray leaves that might have been left in the cave. While awaiting the guide's return, the priest explained the cause of the fellow's sudden disappearance in the morning, which had been to us the cause of so much suffering.

It seemed that the hut in which I was just then resting myself was occupied by an old Arab and his son, who depended for their subsistence on the few sous they received from travellers curious to visit the ruins of the cave, or, as the guides call it, the graves of the Numidian kings. The privilege of conducting travellers through this place was claimed exclusively by them, and rarely indeed did any other Arab venture to trespass on this their domain.

As neither I nor my companion was aware of this pre-emption-right on the part of the inhabitants of the hut, we had gladly accepted the proffered services of the Arab shepherd whom we met as already described. He, desirous of earning a few sous, though he knew he was usurping the office of the legitimate guides, led us into the cave, intending to make use of a torch which he knew was usually deposited by the true guides in a niche at the inner end of the entrance. Arriving there, no torch was to be found; and, fearing that he would lose his promised fee if he explained how matters stood, he left us, without a word of warning, to go and obtain a torch from the old Arab. He hurried to the hut for that purpose; but, unfortunately, both guides were absent just then, and the only course open to him now was to run to the town and get some torches and Bengal lights. He would not tell us what had delayed him, but we could easily conjecture, from the incoherent manner in which he accounted for his absence. The poor devil could obtain no credit, much less the cash wherewith to purchase, until at last, about four o'clock, returning disappointed to the hut, he had recourse to a lie. He told the old Arab, who had by this time got home, that two strangers had been waiting for him the whole morning, to explore the ruins, and that, in his absence, he had undertaken the task, but, finding no torches in the cave, had now come for them. The old man, not having any reason to doubt his story, had furnished him the needed articles; and the reader knows the rest.

Both guides—the pretended as well as the real— were handsomely rewarded by me; for I was heartily glad of the turn of affairs, and even looked back upon the adventure with delight, as something well worth recording. But my poor companion, now that he was relieved from the apprehension of a terrible death, was overwhelmed by grief from another source. The adventure had cost him exceedingly dear. The labor of four weary years had been in great part destroyed during those six terrible hours in the cave, all that he had rescued being some eighty of the paper rolls which had escaped the devouring element. These he carefully unfolded and arranged in book form once more, sighing heavily, as he did so, at the thought of their woeful meagreness and incoherence, and of the time that would be required to get his beloved work once more into shape.

In the year 1854, I was a passenger on one of those magnificent steamers which ply between Louisville and New Orleans, and chanced to meet on board the Reverend Father O——, now one of the most worthy and learned of the bishops who grace the Roman Catholic Church in North America. Upon learning my name, he asked if I had ever travelled in Algiers; and, receiving a reply in the affirmative, he told me that he had been prompted to the inquiry by having seen my name mentioned in the preface of a book entitled "The Historical Biography of St. Augustine," written by Abbé St. Maire and published in Paris in 1851. In the preface the author begs to be excused for the brevity of the biographical portion, assigning as its cause the mishap that befell the original manuscript during an adventure in the ruins of Hippo-Regius at Bona.

The reader, possibly, thinks that I have been somewhat diffuse concerning my under-ground experience; but I can assure him that had he been in our company during those six hours of suspense and suffering, the remembrance of their terrors would be as vivid to him as it now is to me.

Apart from the ruins of Hippo-Regius, Bona deserves to be mentioned on account of the wall that surrounds the town. This wall is thirty feet high, and in some places nine feet thick, and has a circuit of nearly two miles. The coral-fisheries in the Gulf of Bona are also well worthy of notice, and are a source of profit to a large portion of the inhabitants of the town.

At the hotel where I stopped, I happened to meet a Monsieur Lasalle, a member of one of the oldest families of "Bastion de France," a French settlement to the east of the town. This place, he informed me, was often frequented by the coral-fishermen. He was to go thither the next day; and, accepting his kind invitation to accompany him, I set out, on the morrow, for the colony.

This colony has its history. There are still some ruins there, of buildings erected by the Moors or Numidians before the Romans possessed themselves of that part of the country; and the name of many a Roman soldier is yet to be seen chiselled on some time-worn stone or cut into the worm-eaten wood-work. When, in the sixteenth century, the Spaniards invaded Northern Africa, some of the ruins at this place were repaired and rendered habitable by them; and to this day a room is shown to the traveller, in which Barbarossa slept after he had expelled the Spaniards and founded, under the sovereignty of Turkey, the present Algiers.

When Algiers became a source of terror to the Christians on account of its corsairs, this place was for a long time the residence of the chief pirate, and afterwards of his lieutenant, to whom for many years the powers of Europe paid tribute for the protection of their merchant-vessels. In 1816, when Algiers was bombarded by the English fleet under Lord Exmouth, the last of the corsairs, Elim Shein ben Acham, fled hither, dying shortly afterwards, from the effects of the wounds he received during the bombardment; and the place of his interment is still pointed out. After this the place was made a rendezvous by corsairs of less note, until 1830, when the French took possession of the country, and established here their first colony, changing its name to "Bastion de France." At the time of my visit the colony was very prosperous.

The Lasalle family was one of the first to settle in the place. Among the acquaintances whom I formed there was Mademoiselle Hortense Lasalle, a young lady of extremely prepossessing and fascinating manners. She was a Creole, born in the colony, of French parents, and in her disposition were charmingly mingled the vivacity of her nation and the fire of the Moor. She had not seen more than seventeen summers,—but summers of Africa; and she was therefore the full-grown rosebud just opening into maturity.

When my fair young friend learned the object of my visit, she begged me to promise her the first coral that I should gather in the fisheries with my own hands; and I heartily acceded to her request.

Next morning M. Lasalle made me acquainted with an old Arab fisherman, to whom he signified my desire to go on a coral-fishing expedition. The old man promised to gratify me, and, if not able to accompany me himself, to place me in charge of his two sons, Abdul and Giber. The hour for starting was fixed at four o'clock of the afternoon of the same day; and, knowing no better way of passing the intervening time, I returned to spend the hours on the hospitable plantation of my friend, in the charming society of the beautiful hostess,—"la belle Hortense," as she was generally called by her neighbors of the Bastion de France.

Mademoiselle Lasalle, in order to make the time pass as agreeably as possible, proposed a stroll in the neighboring woods; for, as she explained, no stranger ever visited the Bastion without making a pilgrimage to the grave of "La Estrella del Moro,"—"the Star of the Moor." As I had never heard even the name before, I was very willing to learn something of the story and to visit the spot, especially under the guidance of my amiable cicerone. Soon the swift Arabian coursers were carrying us to the place, a distance of some eight miles, which we traversed in about half an hour; and, although myself a native of a country of whose inhabitants it is said that every one is born a horseman, I must admit that in equestrianism the fair Creole was greatly my superior.

The most graphic and facile pen would try in vain to convey an adequate impression of the delightful combination of grace, agility, and swiftness that is witnessed when a handsome Moorish maiden, without a sign of timidity, urges her Arab steed to its swiftest pace. I have at times seen cavalcades of Moorish amazons pass me so rapidly that I have been almost ready to inquire whether it was reality or only a phantom. As with the men, the horse and its fair rider seem one, and the most consummate equestrian skill is exercised with such natural grace as to appear almost instinctive. By the side of my fair companion, I felt not merely awkward, but acknowledged to myself my entire ignorance of the management of the Arabian coursers; for, just as the horse knows its rider, so does it also appear to know when it is guided by a foreign hand; and I was very thankful to arrive at our stopping-place without meeting with some untoward accident.

The animals were placed in charge of a French laborer who belonged to the settlement, while we partook of some refreshment, consisting of peeled Arabian figs, the tunas of South America, commonly known as prickly pears; but those of Africa are entirely different from any I have ever seen elsewhere. They are very large, and exceedingly cooling and refreshing. They grow wild throughout Algeria; and in some parts the French colonists press them, their juice yielding, after fermentation, an excellent wine.

On setting out from the settlement, and during our swift ride, I had asked my fair companion to acquaint me with the object of our pilgrimage; but she obstinately refused to do so until we had arrived on the spot: so that my curiosity was more than usually excited. Huge olive-trees formed the forest, through which a small pathway led to a rocky eminence which we were obliged to ascend. Abandoning myself entirely to the guidance of my fair companion, I was sure that this time I would not be exposed to a repetition of the scene in the cave at Bona, although danger lurked here in another form.

When we had reached the eminence, which was crowned by a grove of olives, we followed a long, winding path to the south side of the hill, where stood a rustic

4

bower of recent structure. Benches were tastefully arranged under its shady roof; and, after we had seated ourselves on one of them, my fair guide did not keep me any longer in suspense, but began her narrative, as follows:—

"My story dates as far back as the sixteenth century. It was at that epoch that the Spaniards, for some cause or other, invaded this part of the country and became its masters.

"Attached to the army of the conqueror was a haughty Aragonian, who obtained leave to separate himself from the main body, and, with a band of lawless desperadoes, whose captain he became, marauded through the country, laying waste the fields, carrying devastation to hut, hamlet, and palace, violating the most sacred rights of humanity, and sparing neither man, woman, nor child.

"The name of this captain was Gonzalez: he was a young Spanish noble, of prepossessing appearance, but of ungovernable passions. He delighted in shedding the blood of the infidels; while to his subordinates he never denied the right of plunder and booty.

"Not far from Bona lived a wealthy Moor, who was celebrated on account of the beauty of the inmates of his harem, which was the largest and most famous in the country. The slave-markets of Morocco, Tunis, and Constantinople had all contributed to it; and occasionally even the corsairs of the Mediterranean ventured into the cities of the Christians and brought some fair damsel as a prize, for which they were liberally rewarded.

"At the time when the Spaniards invaded the country, no one thought they would venture so far into the

interior as Bona, and therefore old Abdul Medshid
gave himself very little uneasiness about what occurred
on the frontier. He lived in his harem, surrounded by
the fairest beauties of all climes, who were condemned
to sacrifice their felicity to his caprices.

"This spot where we now are," continued Mademoiselle Lasalle, "belonged also to Abdul Medshid; and
when the war between the Moors and Spaniards broke
out, Abdul resolved, either from precaution or from
caprice, to build a stronghold on this eminence, which
is screened from our view by the huge olive-trees, but
which, after we have rested from our fatigue, you will
soon behold. Three thousand slaves were brought by
the Moor from his estates in the interior, to build the
stronghold, the plan of which was drawn up by himself, and all the work on which was done under his
personal supervision. The work went on for months;
more slaves were added to the original number, and
yet nothing was seen that would lead the uninitiated to
think that any thing unusual was going on. This eminence, on which the work was executed, remained as
you behold it; not even a tree was displaced: yet it
was certain that more than three thousand slaves were
daily occupied here at hard labor. All that could be
seen by the curious was an insignificant-looking opening on the other side of the hill, into which at daylight
the slaves were driven, and from which at sunset they
emerged; which induced the belief that Abdul Medshid was making a cave wherein to hide his wealth
from the rapacious eye of the invader. But this conjecture was very wide of the mark: Abdul was building a subterranean harem, where he might, in case
of emergency, conceal those beautiful creatures whose

possession had made his name known far and near.
Vessels came down from the Italian coast laden with
marble for this palace; while Tunis and Morocco furnished the interior outfit; and all the booty of the
corsairs was appropriated by Abdul for his palace and
its inmates.

"Years of labor had been spent in its construction;
and at last its completion was signalized by a terrible
sacrifice of human blood; for—so the story goes—
Abdul ordered all the slaves who had worked on it to
be slain, that none might remain to divulge its secrets.
Only two were spared from this massacre, and those
were two old Moors, faithful servants of Abdul's father.
To them was assigned the duty of keeping watch over
the entrance, with orders to put all intruders to death.

"His subterranean palace thus completed, and every
thing arranged which could contribute to the comfort
of its prospective inmates, Abdul calmly awaited the
approach of the Spaniards; and when he heard that
the marauding band of Gonzalez was within four days'
journey, he resolved to transfer his harem to this new
domain.

"In one night, all the inmates of the harem of the
age of twenty or under were taken to the new palace;
while all those who were mothers and over that age
were left behind. Nobody was present at the transfer
except Abdul and his two faithful Moors, who actually
lived at the entrance, near yonder hill, which was the
only passage that led to the palace. Previous to this,
a year's provisions had been accumulated, and every
thing was in readiness to withstand a siege, should it
become necessary.

"The transfer safely effected, and his selected beauties

comfortably installed in their new home, Abdul and his servants walled up the only entrance that led to it, and, covering it with earth and moss, obliterated every external evidence of its existence. A few days later, the two Moors were missing; and it was surmised that they had been slain by the hands of Abdul himself.

"At the time of the first invasion of the Spaniards, there was a grandee of Spain, by name Don José Maria de la Cueva, whose fortune had suffered somewhat in his own country, and who, being young in years and of an adventurous disposition, and, moreover, prompted by the desire to make good his losses, had resolved to follow the army and settle in the newly-conquered territory. His wife, a descendant of one of the most illustrious families of Spain, had departed this life but a short time before, leaving an only child, a lovely daughter, who, at the time of Don José's emigration to the new dominion, was not more than sixteen years of age. Her name was Angela. She was considered beautiful even among the beauties of her own people; and so remarkable was her appearance that she was very generally known by the *sobriquet* of ' La Estrella' (the star). Her father had brought with him the remnant of his fortune, which, in their new home, was sufficient to enable him to lead a life appropriate to his rank.

" La Estrella, as Angela was called, was overjoyed at the idea of the change of scene; and soon after their arrival, both father and daughter were comfortably settled in a castle not far from Oran,—a property that had belonged to a wealthy Moor who had incurred the displeasure of the Spanish conqueror, and whose entire family had perished with him, with the exception of one son who was fortunate enough to escape. Don

José, by a decree of the crown, took possession of the Moorish castle, and soon transformed it into a residence fit for a Spanish grandee, and lived there as comfortably as he could have done in his native country,— nay, with even greater ease and state than he had ever before enjoyed. Some soldiers detached from the army remained with him, and they, settling down on the lands which belonged to the castle, formed there the first Spanish settlement in that part of the country.

"Every thing went on as happily as could be desired; and even the fear of molestation by marauding bands of Kabyls soon vanished, for months had passed and not even a strange face was to be met with in or near the domains of the castle. Don José abandoned himself to the enjoyment of perfect ease and comfort, and to the education of his only child, La Estrella, who, as she grew up, became still more beautiful than she had been in early girlhood. She often took rides in the neighboring woods, which, far removed as she was from the scenes of civilization, served her as recreation; while in the evenings, and especially after sunset, she would frequently stroll through the neighborhood, sometimes visiting the small farm-houses belonging to the soldiers who had settled on her father's estate.

"Among these people, La Estrella was as the apparition of a beautiful star, for she always had something in store for them, and during their sicknesses she was their ministering angel. Every one in the neighborhood knew her; every one respected and loved her; and any misfortune that happened to her was felt by the whole community.

"One day when she had fallen from her wild Arabian steed and was obliged to keep her room, she was missed by the neighbors; they besieged the castle from morning until night, to ascertain the state of her health and whether she would soon be able to appear among them again: so accustomed were they to see her bright and beautiful face that they felt her absence when a couple of days had elapsed without their seeing her.

"Don José had already resided over eight months on his new domains. The settlement was prospering, and nothing as yet had occurred to blight his brilliant hopes for the future, when one day La Estrella, who had taken her customary walk, remained absent longer than usual. The evening was far advanced; the night, that wrapped every thing around in the deepest obscurity, had augmented its dark mantle by the threatening appearance of heavy and stormy clouds; a tornado such as is never witnessed in any other part of the world was approaching; the thunder announced its coming by low, ominous mutterings, and now and then a flash of lightning would rend the dense clouds: it was the forerunner of the simoom. All the domestic animals, warned by instinct of the coming danger, had already sought shelter; while every human being accustomed to that fearful war of the elements took refuge in the remotest seclusion of his abode; for no one dared to brave in the open field the fiery breath of the storm. In the castle of Don José all was consternation; for La Estrella had not yet made her appearance, and, if she were overtaken by the simoom, her fate was sealed. Her father became frantic; the servants of the household ran to and fro in the wildest confusion; all offered their services, but no one ventured into the open air, until Don José, beside himself with apprehension, rushed from the castle, followed by all the male domestics, to brave the danger of the elements, in search of the beloved Estrella. As they mingled their cries with the roar of the thunder, above all others was heard the voice of the bereaved father, calling, in heart-rending tones, upon his Estrella, his darling child.

"Nearer and nearer came the fearful simoom : its fiery and suffocating breath could already be felt. Some of the domestics were returning, unable to withstand its baleful influence; while others were endeavoring to persuade their master to expose himself no longer to the rage of the elements, in a hopeless search for the lost one. But he heeded them not : tearing his hair and beating his breast, he rushed wildly onward, until, overcome by the stifling atmosphere, he fell exhausted to the ground. As he lay there, unable to move, and a prey to the keenest anguish, it seemed to him that a cavalcade on fiery coursers was passing close by. The riders were all black; but one of them seemed to carry, clasped in his arms, a woman who lay across the steed, with dishevelled hair and flowing robe. He thought it was his beloved child; and, screaming, 'Estrella! Estrella!' his senses failed him, and he saw no more.

"That night, the storm that had threatened in the evening made fearful havoc throughout the land : trees were uprooted, houses were blown down, herds of cattle that failed to reach a shelter were scattered and destroyed, and—by what accident was never ascertained— the castle of Don José was burned to the ground. The next day nothing but the smoking ruins remained to tell the sad tale: all its inmates had perished, and a heap of blackened stones and smouldering ruins was all that remained of what had yesterday been the happy home of the father and his child.

"Some days afterwards, a haggard, wretched-looking man was seen hovering around the ruins; his dress was torn, his walk feeble and uncertain, his gaze that of a maniac. He spoke to no one, answered none; but in piteous tones and with heart-rending sobs he constantly gave utterance to two words:—'My Estrella!'

"At the time of the above occurrence, Gonzalez the marauder, with his band, was in the neighborhood of Oran; and, hearing of the misfortune that had befallen his countryman Don José de la Cueva, he resolved to visit the spot which had been the scene of so terrible a calamity, and to endeavor to find a clue to the whereabouts of La Estrella; for some curious stories were in circulation as to the cause of her disappearance. The Spanish colonists in the neighborhood had become greatly alarmed, for the abduction of the girl and the destruction of her father's castle appeared to be the work of one and the same hand; and it was resolved to leave no means untried to trace the crime home to its perpetrator and his accessories and punish them as they deserved.

"Gonzalez and his band soon arrived at the place where but a few days before had stood the stately dwelling of their countryman; and, lawless and hard-hearted though they were, the sight of the ruins of what had so lately been a happy home filled every heart with feelings of compassion. In vain did they look for some one whom they might question concerning the fate of the unfortunate inmates: all that remained to denote the former presence of human beings was the charred bones that here and there were discovered among the heaps of stones and ashes.

"While gazing on the scene, absorbed in thought,

Gonzalez noticed, not far from where he stood, a slight motion in some rubbish among the ruins. He directed some of his men to investigate the cause; when, lifting up a heavy flagstone which seemed to have been designed as a shelter from the burning rays of the sun, they beheld a sight that caused them for a moment to recoil. It was the figure of a man, but of one who had all the appearance of an inmate of the grave. His dishevelled white hair gave to his smoke-blackened face a ghastly appearance. Around one arm was tied a broad red ribbon, which he seemed to treasure; for as soon as he beheld the men who had intruded upon his retreat he sought to protect it with his free hand, and screamed, in piteous tones, 'Oh, do not take it from me! it is all that is left to me of my Estrella!'

"Gonzalez and his comrades looked on this sad spectacle for some minutes in silence and with uncovered heads, touched with feelings of the deepest commiseration; for in the wretched maniac before them they recognized their unfortunate countryman the father of Estrella. After the impression of the moment had in some degree passed away, the leader addressed several questions to the miserable being; but to no purpose: reason had fled forever, and to every question was returned the one mournful answer,—'Estrella!'

"Not wishing to remain any longer where all that he beheld excited such painful thoughts, Gonzalez called his men together and made them promise to avenge the wrongs of their countryman, and never to sheathe their swords until they had restored to the unhappy father his beloved daughter. As with one voice they repeated the oath administered by their captain; and then, taking Don José with them, they

galloped away from the spot that had impressed them
with such unwonted grief and sadness. From that
day Gonzalez changed his name: he was no longer the
'Captain of the Fearless Band,' but 'The Avenger of
La Estrella.'

"During the night following the destruction of the
home of the Spanish grandee, a cavalcade of Moorish
horsemen drew up before the castle of Abdul Medshid.
The chief of the band demanded to be admitted; and,
giving his name to the sentinel, he was soon afterwards
ushered into the presence of the master. His comrades
did not have to wait long; for soon he reappeared,
carrying a heavy bag of gold, which he handed to one
of his followers; then, going towards the centre of the
group, he lifted a muffled form from one of the horses,
and carried it into the castle, where he delivered it into
the charge of a servant. Immediately afterwards he
retired, and, mounting his steed, hurried away with his
band.

"It was a beautiful night. Not a leaf was stirring;
and the balmy odors of flowers loaded the serene atmosphere. The lights in the castle of Abdul Medshid
were extinguished, and its inmates were all, apparently,
wrapped in slumber. The eunuchs, placed like faithful
watchdogs at the doors of the various apartments, lay
stretched in sleep, as though the universal calm had
made them forget their duty of incessant vigilance.
But there was one whose eyes were not visited by the
drowsy god: the master of the castle was restless: he
alone could not sleep.

"In the innermost apartment of his stronghold, on
a divan of the softest cushions, lay a human form.
The white cashmere mantle that enfolded it did not

conceal the luxuriant but dishevelled masses of dark
hair that covered the head; while a bared arm revealed
a hand which, while it seemed too small to be a woman's,
was yet too large to be that of a child. The face was
hidden by a veil; and the gentle and regular motion
of the beautifully rounded bosom alone gave evidence
that life was not extinct.

"In front of the divan stood the tall figure of Abdul
Medshid. A snow-white turban, in whose centre
gleamed a massive diamond, covered his head; his
scimitar, closely set with brilliants, hung loosely at his
side; a cashmere tunic of the finest texture invested
his form; while his sandals were covered with precious
stones whose lustre rivalled that of the gems with
which his girdle was thickly studded.

"Holding in one hand a richly-chased golden lamp,
whose light was fed from a precious oil that filled the
air with aromatic odor as it burned, he bent over the
seemingly sleeping form; while with the other hand
he raised the veil that covered the face. No sooner
had he beheld the features than he started back in
astonishment; a cry of joy burst from his lips, and the
fair sleeper awoke, gazing around her in a bewilderment not like that which is often witnessed in one
aroused from a transient slumber, but rather like the
lethargic stupor produced by a powerful narcotic
draught. Abdul Medshid stood as though transfixed.
He saw before him a face and form such as he had
never hitherto beheld save in imagination,—such as he
had believed could belong only to one of those fair
celestial beings of whom the devout Mohammedan
dreams as his richest guerdon in Paradise. It was no
dream: those features, he knew, belonged to a living

form: yet it seemed to him that he must touch her, must hear her voice, before he should be entirely convinced that the beauty on which his eyes feasted was not the creature of his imagination, liable to be dispelled by a breath.

"Impelled by this feeling of wonder, Abdul advanced towards the divan, every feature and motion expressive of the deepest reverence and astonishment. The half-dreaming and bewildered girl, as he approached, gazed at him with that agonizing look which is so often witnessed at the bedside of the dying, when it would seem as if the soul desired to take in at one earnest glance all that remains of earthly life. For an instant only did she manifest even this consciousness of his presence: as he came nearer she again fell into the death-like stupor from which but a moment before she had been aroused. Kneeling at her side, he gazed intently at the motionless figure; he raised her arm and placed it on the divan; he pressed his lips to her hand, and touched the luxuriant curls of jet-black hair which enshrined her lovely face. Laying his ear to her bosom and listening to the throbbing of her heart, he knew that what he saw and felt was a blessed reality, that life was not extinct, and that the strange stupor he witnessed was merely the effect of some powerful narcotic administered by those who had brought him this pearl beyond all price. Then, addressing the still unconscious form, he involuntarily exclaimed, 'By what name, O most beautiful of thy sex, art thou called?'

" * * * The hour was long past midnight; the moon had hidden herself behind a passing cloud, and the dim light of the stars was all that illumined the

5

path that winds from yonder vale to the foot of the
eminence where we are now seated. Now and then the
queen of night, as if prompted by curiosity, peeped
through a rift in the cloud which had obscured her,
and darted a ray of light on the figure of a man,
heavily burdened, who was bending his steps in the
direction of this hill, from the castle of the far-famed
Abdul Medshid. His progress was but slow; for
every now and then he stopped, whether to recover
from fatigue or to listen for the sound of pursuit it was
impossible to determine. At last, however, he reached
the eminence; whereupon, depositing his burden carefully upon the ground, he drew from under his mantle
a long silken cord, which he tied around the seemingly
inanimate figure: then, taking it once more in his
arms, he resumed his journey, pressing on until he
reached a huge olive-tree, the tallest and sturdiest of
the grove, whose majestic dimensions had caused it to
be known among the inhabitants of the vicinity as the
'father of the forest.' It was of immense diameter,
and was revered for its age and for the shelter which
its noble branches afforded. That tree was hollowed
in the centre; and two persons could with ease have
been concealed in the cavity of its trunk.

"Just as he arrived at that spot, the moon, hitherto
obscured, shone forth in all its glory, making every
object visible. And there, on his knees, bending over
the still inanimate form of La Estrella (for she it was
who had been brought to his castle by the midnight
cavalcade), was Abdul Medshid, who had now come to
place the beautiful Christian maiden in the under-
ground harem of his marble palace. That tree was
the only entrance to the subterranean domain of the

Moor, and the secret was known to no one but himself. What mechanism was contained in the hollow of the olive is unknown; but certain it is that by its means he was enabled to communicate with the inmates of the harem at any hour, without the remotest danger of detection. Here, then, Abdul and his burden vanished from sight.

"To the southwest of Algiers, in the province of Oran, and about three miles from the city of that name, lies a small place called Marsa-el-Kebir, the *Portus Magnus* of the ancients. At the time of the occurrence which I have just related, this place was little better than a nest of corsairs; and after the Spanish occupation, the harbor being excellent, many of the smaller native craft gathered there, ostensibly for purposes of trade, but in reality for piracy and all kinds of unlawful traffic. It was also the rendezvous of many so-called fishermen, who were sufficiently cautious to avoid arousing the suspicions of the not over-watchful Spanish authorities.

"At that time Don Mariano Miraflores had command of the place,—a position which gave him very little trouble, since the only quarter from which an attack could be looked for was the sea; and, as the Spanish government always had a number of war-vessels cruising in the roadstead, it was very improbable that the unsubdued Moors, who were deprived of all naval war material, would molest the town from that direction. Being a dissolute and licentious man, the governor gave himself up to a life of the most reckless debauchery, and surrounded himself with a large number of beautiful Moorish girls, whom he had taken from the nomadic Arabs in skirmishes in which victory

had favored him. Under the pretext of retaliation for
pretended wrongs, also, he often dragged young maidens
from their parental roof; and soon his palace presented
the appearance of a harem.

"Although the natives,—Arabs, Moors, and Kabyls,
—overawed by the vastly superior force of their conquerors, submitted in silence to these outrages, they
cherished the most rebellious and revengeful feelings
towards the invaders, and each succeeding day intensi-
fied their hatred of the Christians, as they witnessed
the indignities offered to them on the soil which their
ancestors had trodden in freedom.

"Nor were the soldiers of Miraflores one whit better
than their master: night after night the commandant's
palace was the scene of the wildest orgies, in which the
licentious chief joined as heartily as the most reckless
of his subordinates.

"Among the natives, the Arabs considered themselves the aristocrats, and this claim was tacitly acknowledged by the other races, the Moors and Kabyls:
so that, whenever a revolt occurred, it was always an
Arab who was suspected of being the instigator, an
Arab who was the leader, and, when the authorities
had quelled the disturbance, it was upon the Arab
population that the punishment fell. Yet, despite the
persistent humiliation and cruel treatment to which
they were subjected by their conquerors, the spirit of
the Arabs remained unbroken, and it required incessant
vigilance on the part of the Christians to avoid the
snares laid for them at almost every step by the wily
hand of the infidel.

"Don Mariano Miraflores, under the pretext of
having detected a conspiracy which, he asserted, had

been connived at by a wealthy Moor who lived in the neighborhood of Marsa-el-Kebir, surprised the castle of the latter one night, carrying off as trophies the women of his harem, to add to the number already in his own seraglio. In vain did the Moor protest his innocence of the alleged conspiracy and offer to prove his fidelity to the crown of Spain and his entire submission to her laws; fruitless were all his entreaties for the restoration of his women. Nothing that he could say or do had any effect on the brutal governor: he had long coveted the Moor's treasures, and neither money nor prayers could induce him to relinquish his grasp.

"This last act of flagrant injustice had filled to overflowing the cup of bitterness; and as he who had suffered the wrong was looked upon by the natives as their superior, being a man of rank and influence, they were ready to aid him, even to the sacrifice of their lives, in any undertaking to avenge himself upon the Christian ruler.

"As I have already remarked, Marsa-el-Kebir was the place where the poorer class of the natives carried on their trade as fishermen, for here they found a ready market: hence the gathering of a large number of fishing-boats and their crews in and around the harbor excited no suspicion on the part of the Spanish population of the town.

"One evening, a fortnight after that on which the cavalcade had halted before the castle of Abdul Medshid and left with him the precious treasure in the person of La Estrella, the harbor of Marsa-el-Kebir was unusually lively. It was the feast-day of Santa Barbara, the patron saint of the soldiery of his Most

Christian Majesty the King of Spain. It was observed as a holiday by the entire Christian population; while the natives, by no means with willing hearts, but merely to avoid incurring the displeasure of their masters, mingled freely with the Christians, and to all outward appearance joined in the festivities with as much zest as the Spaniards. No soldier but would have considered it a species of sacrilege to remain sober on that day; while the civilians, in greater or less degree, took part in the general debauchery. The better class of the population had assembled at the palace of the governor, who on such an auspicious occasion was unusually generous in the dispensation of his favors. The fishermen from the coast, who, as a special mark of respect for their ruler, had donned their gayest attire, had also congregated in large numbers, and fraternized most heartily with the intoxicated people. All was enjoyment and revelry, the Christians seeming to have completely forgotten that they were surrounded by their deadly foes, who only awaited the opportunity to strike a blow that should carry terror into the hearts of the invaders.

"In many of the fishing-boats moored around the wharf were strange faces, which at any other time than this would have attracted attention; but now, in the festivity which reigned, the circumstance passed unnoticed. But had a careful observer been present, he would have heard every now and then something that sounded like a password or a countersign, which ran like wildfire from one to another, until it was known to every man of the native population. Nor were words the only means of communication: signs were exchanged, which doubtless bore a deep significance to those who received them.

" All these signs and watchwords evidently came from one source, and seemed to proceed from an insignificant-looking lad, who, judging from his shabby dress, belonged to the poorest class of fishermen. He was leaning carelessly against a post on the pier, or mole, seemingly thinking of nothing but the enjoyment of his evening repast, which consisted of a piece of dried fish, and of which he was partaking as though he had eaten nothing for several days. On a closer examination, however, it would have been found that his features were not those of the low class of Arabs denoted by his dress, but bespoke a higher rank : they were, in fact, those of the young man who had delivered to Abdul Medshid, on the eventful night which I have already described, the daughter of the unhappy Don José, and who for his services had received so rich a reward in gold.

" Melech-el-Hachem, the youth in question, was the only son of that Moor who at the beginning of the Spanish invasion had perished with his whole household, and whose domain had been ceded by the crown to the Spanish grandee Don José Maria de la Cueva, the father of La Estrella. This youth had been out hunting on the day of the massacre of his father's family ; and to that circumstance alone did he owe his life. When, on his return from the chase, he beheld the hated symbol of the Christian planted on one of the towers that graced his father's castle, he had no difficulty in divining the fate that had befallen his kindred. For weeks afterwards he wandered about the mountains in the neighborhood of the castle, not daring to show himself near it ; and having had his surmises as to his parent's sad fate fully confirmed by a wandering

Arab who had also been fortunate enough to escape
the sword of the conqueror, he resolved to abandon the
vicinity entirely, and to seek refuge, with his new companion, in the distant mountains. There they soon
met others who had fled from the persecutions of the
invaders.

"Melech and his companions now entered into a
solemn compact, and swore by Allah and his prophet
to wreak summary vengeance on the Christian dogs
who had deprived them of all that was dear on earth
Melech was unanimously chosen chief of the band;
and, considering the force at his disposal too small to
operate with any hope of success against the disciplined
Spanish soldiery, he resolved to make the new pos-
sessor of his father's domains the first victim in retaliation for the cruel fate of his family. The most effective
blow he could strike would be to gain possession of the
daughter of the Spaniard; and, having determined
upon this, he absented himself from the place, where
detection would have been almost certain, resolved to
return at a more convenient season.

"Eight months had elapsed, and, as I have said, the
settlement established by Don José was prospering: no
foe had been seen near the place, to excite even suspicion, until that fatal evening when the very elements
seemed to have conspired to assist in the execution
of the evil designs of the implacable enemy of the
Christian.

"It was Melech-el-Hachem who avenged the death
of his father. He consigned his parental domain to
the flames, rather than leave it in the possession of the
foreign despoiler; while with his own hands he carried
off the beautiful Estrella, waylaying her in one of her

customary visits to the neighbors, and, in a spirit of revenge which would have considered her death an insufficient expiation, sold her to a life of shame, in the harem of Abdul Medshid.

"Before Estrella had left her native home, and a short time after her mother's death, her father had given her a medallion in which was enclosed the likeness of his wife. This medallion was, next to her father, the dearest object of the young girl's heart, and she wore it constantly, by day and by night. On the night when she was abducted from her home it was taken from her. That was all that her abductor claimed as his reward: the gold that he received from Abdul Medshid he gave to be divided among his companions; but that likeness of Estrella's mother he carried with him as an amulet, to remind him of the oath he had now partially fulfilled,—namely, to avenge his murdered father and his desolated home.

"After this, the young Melech-el-Hachem left the vicinity and proceeded with his followers to another part of the country, near Marsa-el-Kebir, where a distant relative of his father resided; and a few days after his arrival he witnessed the outrage committed by Don Mariano Miraflores which I have already narrated.

"It was he who urged the old Moor to revenge; and, being filled with hatred towards his Christian foe, he organized the plan and was intrusted with its execution.

"The young fisherman in the harbor of Marsa-el-Kebir, whom we have seen quietly issuing his commands to his people, on the evening of the feast in honor of Santa Barbara, was none other than Melech-el-Hachem.

"The night was already far advanced. Bonfires were burning here and there, around which the drunken soldiery were dancing in wild excitement. The noise of revelry from the palace, mingling with the wild and fantastic war-songs of the soldiers, showed that all were wrapped in a feeling of entire security.

"Statue-like stood the young fisherman, in the same place where, some hours before, he was partaking of his evening meal. The greater part of his companions had by his command scattered themselves through the various streets, mingling with the soldiery on the friendliest terms; and many a bumper was emptied by Christian and infidel together, as if naught but harmony prevailed. No one would have imagined, to witness the scene, that any thing else than good feeling existed between the various members of the excited crowds that seemed wholly bent on hilarious enjoyment.

"Suddenly another word of command was uttered by the hitherto impassive-looking young Arab. That word flew with lightning speed, and by the time it had reached the ear of all who understood its meaning, bonfires of a different kind from those of the early part of the evening were kindled, this time not in honor of the Christian, but in announcement of the terrible infidel avenger.

"In one instant the whole town of Marsa-el-Kebir was enveloped in flames, whose fiery arms spread far and wide, embracing all within their burning grasp.

"In the tumult that ensued, the scimitar was not idle. Guided by a cool and practised leader, and fired by the memory of their wrongs, the assailants met with but slight resistance from the unprepared Spaniards. The humble fisherman had left his post; the mask was thrown off; and with unsheathed sword he led his faithful band to the bloody onslaught, sparing none who bore the name of Christian.

"With a few followers who, like himself, had personal wrongs to avenge, he made his way to the palace of the Christian commander, leaving the rest to continue the work of general slaughter. But here he found no easy task. The inmates, startled from their midnight revelries by the consternation that prevailed without, sprang to their feet, resolved to defend their lives to the last extremity, and, provided with weapons from the palace armory, they kept the foe in check until the entrance was secured. The danger to which they were exposed sobered them, and caused them to strain every nerve in their efforts for defence; for well they knew the fate that awaited them should they be overcome. Fortunate was it for them that they succeeded in arresting their besiegers so soon; for had they been a few minutes later, not a Christian would have escaped to tell the tale. Inspired with a demoniac fury, the Arabs rushed towards the palace. Men and women, old and young, each with some wrong to avenge, thronged around the building where their oppressors were besieged; while the more rapacious scoured the town in search of plunder. Loud above the uproar of the excited multitude around the palace, was heard the commanding voice of the young Arab, the abductor of Estrella.

"The besieged, however, presented an undaunted front. The walls were thick, and not liable to the ravages of the flames; while through the openings many an arquebuse, directed by a Christian hand, sent messengers of death to the infidel.

"As the hours advanced, the fury of the foe increased. They now resolved to try another plan. Combustibles of all descriptions were brought by the enraged throng and piled around the place; the torch was applied, and a fiery girdle soon encircled the palace with its handful of brave defenders.

"It was not hard to foresee their end; but they scorned to yield, for well they knew the fate that awaited them at the hands of their ruthless foes. Mercy they could not expect; for when had the Christian been known to have mercy when the bleeding Arab lay at his feet?

"The flames were already making an impression on the gate of the palace: in a few moments it must yield and give admittance to the infuriated assailants. As a last effort at defence, a cruel expedient was resorted to. Among the inmates of the palace were some Arab women, who had been taken from the different tribes, some for lust and others as hostages, and all of whom belonged to the seraglio of the Christian commander. They were now brought forth and placed where the shower of missiles fell thickest. As soon as the besiegers saw this living breastwork composed of women of their own creed and nation, they simultaneously ceased their onslaught, and awaited the further commands of their leader. Melech-el-Hachem stood bewildered. He could not command the slaughter of his own race, and even had he ordered it, no Arab would have raised an arm. However, more combustibles were added to the flames, in order to hasten the destruction of the entrance.

"When the Christians saw the happy result of their strategy, they directed their attention to the defence

of the main point of attack,—the principal entrance,—
which was just about to give way. They strengthened
it by hurriedly throwing up an inner barricade of stone
and earth, and by this means hoped to be able to delay
the fatal moment. At the same time they threatened
to sacrifice all the captives to the flames if the fire were
not immediately extinguished. This threat not having
the desired effect, one of the women was precipitated
into the flames that were consuming the main entrance.
Horror-struck, the besiegers recoiled at the sight;
and, ere another victim could be immolated, they extinguished the fire, looking to their leader to devise
some more effective plan for the reduction of the
Christians.

"They hurriedly gathered around their chief, who
at that moment heard a sound that chilled his very
blood; and, ere he could communicate his fears to his
bewildered followers, the band of Gonzalez, the avenger
of La Estrella, was upon them.

"It seems that, unknown to Melech-el-Hachem,
Gonzalez, with his band, had been encamped at some
distance from the town, yet not so far but that he could
see the flames, as they rose in fitful starts, as if calling
to the rescue. Accustomed to such scenes, he quickly
surmised the cause. To mount was the work of a moment; and, dashing with all the speed of their fiery
coursers to the place of action, they arrived at the town
just as the tumult had reached its height. With a
wild shout of 'To the rescue!' they charged furiously
upon the astonished Arabs; and terrible was the havoc
that ensued. And now from the palace rushed the
handful of men who had so bravely withstood the
siege, and, joining those who had so unexpectedly come

to their assistance, took an active part in the work of
slaughter.

"The blood of the unhappy Arabs flowed in tor-
rents; while the groans of the wounded and the dying
rent the air on every side.

"Melech-el-Hachem, the leader of the Arabs, far
from being daunted by the terrible odds against him,
fought bravely and desperately. Wherever the battle
was fiercest, there was he to be found in the foremost
ranks, encouraging his followers, by voice and example,
to slay the 'Christian dogs.' But at last, overpowered
and wounded, he fell; and his followers fled in dismay
before the determined onslaught of the Christians.

"The revolt having been quelled, and order restored,
the young Arab chief was pointed out to Gonzalez as
the leader of the rebellious natives; and by his direction he was taken under a strong escort to the palace,
there to await the order of the commander: for, as he
reasoned, nothing could be gained by slaying him;
while, if he were spared, a clue might be discovered
to the secret springs of the revolt which had so suddenly broken out, and which might extend throughout
the land.

"The next morning, Melech-el-Hachem was led into
the presence of Gonzalez. The wound which he had
received was not mortal; but he was weak from loss of
blood. He stood erect in the presence of his captor:
the death which he felt awaited him had no terrors
for his proud spirit. The Spanish chieftain put many
questions to him, but could elicit nothing. 'Melech-
el-Hachem is no traitor,' was the Arab's proud response.
'I am ready to meet death, in whatever form it may
come: it is therefore idle to ask me to betray my

brethren. No true believer in the prophet would sell his kindred,—no, not for all the gold in Christendom.'

"'Thy life shall be spared, and all that thou hast lost be restored to thee, if thou wilt but confess,' said Gonzalez.

"'Thou knowest not the noble Arab's son. Among those of thy creed such base merchandise may be found; but to the Arab, life is worthless when honor has departed.'

"'In sooth,' sneered Gonzalez, 'to hear an Arab speak thus, one might imagine that honor is not unknown to thee.'

"As Gonzalez uttered these words, the pale cheek of the young Arab flushed deeply, and he replied, 'Thou dost not believe in the Arab's honor? Thou sayest well; for never hast thou heard it mentioned. And why? Because with the Arab honor and existence are identical: separate them, and he no longer lives. The Christian's honor is an article of merchandise, brought into the market and sold to the highest bidder. And thou, the leader of such men as compose thy robber band,—how canst thou speak of honor?'

"Stung to fury, Gonzalez refused to listen any longer, and directed that the Arab be taken at once from his presence. At that moment, however, he noticed around the neck of the prisoner a red ribbon, to which was attached a glittering object; and, curious to know what it contained, he ordered one of his men to bring it to him for inspection. The Arab refused to yield it; but resistance was in vain against the ferocious grasp of the soldiers, who, wresting the amulet from him, handed it to the captain.

"Scarcely had Gonzalez opened the medallion, when

a death-like pallor overspread his countenance, and his powerful frame shook with nervous excitement. Long and intently did he gaze upon it, every moment adding to his bewilderment.

"'Stop!' he called at last to the infidel. 'How hast thou come by this relic?' A bitter smile played around the lips of the young Arab; for, by the troubled gaze and agitated frame of Gonzalez, he was convinced that some tender cord had been rudely touched in the Christian's heart. 'One victim more,' thought he, 'to avenge my father's death.'

"'Wilt thou confess?' shouted Gonzalez, enraged by the triumphant look of the Arab.

"'What am I to confess?' calmly replied young Melech. 'Dost thou wish me to declare whence I obtained the medallion? Whence hast thou the many brilliants that decorate thy breast? From the victims of thy blood-stained hands; from the infidel, as thou art pleased to call us. Know, then, that from the Christian I have mine.'

"'But,' resumed Gonzalez, 'tell me the name of him from whom thou hast taken this.'

"'The name!' said Melech. 'Askest thou the infidel's name before thy murderous weapon pierces his defenceless breast?'

"Convulsively Gonzalez grasped the hilt of his sword, and for a moment seemed as though he were about to run the weapon through the body of his dauntless prisoner; but, suddenly recalling himself to reason, he directed that Melech be taken back to his cell.

"Long before the sun had dispelled the dark mantle of the following night, a cavalcade of horsemen was travelling along the road that leads northward from the town of Mersa.

"That troop was headed by the well-known Gonzalez, who was conducting his followers on a somewhat mysterious expedition. Without allowing them any rest after the exhaustion consequent upon the combat with the rebellious Arabs, he had informed them that their presence was needed at another place of action; and, after making the necessary preparations, he pressed onward as if the object of this expedition were of greater importance than even the service in which he was engaged for the King of Spain.

"His troop, while not so large as usual, consisted exclusively of men who had seen hard fighting, either in their native land or on the conquered soil of Algiers. They were not remarkable for cleanliness; but their swords were keen and bright, and their steeds in condition for a long and arduous journey.

"In their midst were two horsemen, both seeming to be carefully guarded. One of them sat bent on his steed, which, without any guidance from the bridle, moved as if instinctively aware that its rider was indifferent as to the course it took; and, indeed, but for the regular movement of his body produced by the motion of the horse, one might have supposed that the rider was asleep. His head, bent forward on his breast, was covered with a jipi-japa (sun-hat), while underneath hung disordered locks of white and grayish hair. His features were those of one who, by some great disaster, has suffered in a single night the grief and anguish of a lifetime. From his face the muscles seemed to have disappeared; while the skin, closely adhering to the bones, gave them an unnatural appearance of prominence. The deeply-sunken cavities of the eye imparted a spectral look to the eyeball. The whole frame was emaciated to the last degree; and the arms and legs hung listlessly from the body. Around his right arm was tied a faded red ribbon. That sad wreck of humanity was all that remained of the former Spanish grandee, the once happy father of La Estrella. Although far from being a prisoner, he was constantly watched by the band of Gonzalez, since at every opportunity he would escape from his guard; and, as the captain desired to have him constantly by his side, as a clue to the cause of the mysterious disappearance of La Estrella, he had placed him in charge of his men, knowing that he would be treated with all the respect due to his former position and his present misfortune.

"The appearance of the other horseman was in striking contrast with that of the wretched maniac. Young and vigorous, he bestrode his charger with as haughty an air as though he were the commander of the troop; and, indeed, but for the shackles that bound his hands and feet, it might have been supposed, from his proud bearing, that, if not the commander, he was at least a person of high rank and dignity.

"And, in fact, notwithstanding the chains that shackled his limbs and the sneers and gibes of the guard, Melech-el-Hachem was a man of dignity and rank.

"His father, at the time of the Spanish invasion, was governor of the province, and one of the highest dignitaries of the realm. At the beginning of the war he had raised a force of eight thousand men, levied entirely from his own domains, clothed, subsisted, and paid by himself, and had bravely fought at their head. Fortune, however, was adverse, and he was severely punished by the conqueror for his fidelity to his country. His castles and domains were confiscated, and he and his entire household put to death, with the exception of the only heir, Melech-el-Hachem.

"Side by side rode the young Arab and the maniac, without knowing any thing of the history of each other. Gonzalez himself was not aware of the part the prisoner had played in the carrying away of La Estrella, to find some trace of whom was the principal object of his present expedition.

"The medallion which he had taken from the Arab, and which enclosed a miniature portrait of the mother of La Estrella, whom he had known in his native land, led him to suspect that Melech was in some way connected with the abduction; but there was no certainty as to the matter. The Arab steadily refused to divulge any thing; for the torment he caused the captain by his silence was a sweet morsel to him who had so much to revenge.

"In vain did Gonzalez show the medallion to the maniac: he looked at it with a vacant stare; and the mention of his lost daughter appeared to excite no interest. Now and then, indeed, he muttered the name of Estrella, but in a mechanical way and as though the word conveyed no idea to his darkened mind.

"Nevertheless, the medallion was a clue; and Gonzalez still hoped to make it the means of eventually clearing up the mystery. It was his intention to take Don José back to the spot where once had stood his happy home, trusting that the associations of the locality, in conjunction with the image of his departed wife, would bring back a lucid interval, however brief, during which he might ascertain something that would aid him in discovering the whereabouts of the lost girl.

" During the tedious journey, Melech-el-Hachem held converse with no one. His proud bearing remained unchanged; and not a sound escaped his lips, except that now and then, as the troop rode in sight of some stately Moorish castle, from whose towers waved the standard of the conqueror, his breast would heave with a deep sigh. But even then he would endeavor to repress his emotion, lest his foe should have occasion to exult over his grief.

" At last they reached their journey's end, halting in a hamlet a short distance from the ruins of Don José's castle.

" The occupants of this hamlet were Arabs of the nomadic tribe, who, like the gipsies, take possession of every unoccupied dwelling they find in their wanderings, and lay claim to every thing that has no visible owner.

" The night had far advanced; and on the floor of the hamlet the imprisoned heir of the former owner of all the lands around lay calmly sleeping. In front of the entrance blazed a large fire, around which the soldiers had bivouacked, chatting familiarly with the Arab gipsies.

" But the leader of the band was absent. Revolving in his mind his numerous plans for future operations, Gonzalez had mechanically directed his steps towards the spot where, some time before, among the then smoking ruins, he had met the maniac, La Estrella's father.

"Seating himself on a heap of blackened stones, he gave himself up to earnest meditation as to the best means of obtaining a clue to the fate of La Estrella. The more he reflected, however, the more hopeless appeared the task. Of but one thing did he feel assured, —that the young Arab prisoner could, if he chose, disclose the secret. Wearied at last by his fruitless attempts to clear up the mystery, he rose, and, after a mournful look at the ruins, prepared to go back to the hamlet. The path that he now took wound through a thicket, which had grown so luxuriantly as to render the passage difficult. He stepped aside to find some opening, but suddenly stopped; for it seemed to him that he heard a slight rustling close at hand. Hastily concealing himself in the dark shadows of the foliage, he eagerly awaited the approach of the midnight wanderer. At that moment, with a step like that of the frighted fawn, there emerged from the bush a young Arab girl, whom, on his arrival at the hamlet, he had noticed as belonging to the gipsies.

"Quick as thought he grasped the arm of the startled wanderer, and demanded what errand had brought her out at that late hour. Frightened at the unexpected apparition, and recognizing the captain of the band, she supposed all was known to him. Sinking on her knees, she entreated him to spare her life. But Gonzalez, as we are aware, knew nothing. The extraordinary conduct of the maiden excited his suspicions; for what had she to fear from the captain of the band who were bivouacked among her own people? At first he was puzzled how to frame his questions so as not to betray his ignorance of her errand. 'Confess all,' he said, 'and I will spare thy life.' The frightened girl

immediately revealed her secret; and Gonzalez learned
that, while the soldiers were listening to the entertain-
ing stories of the Arabs, one of the latter, unseen by the
guard, had stealthily approached the prisoner and from
him received a message to be delivered to Abdul Medshid, the owner of La Estrella. This message was
intrusted to the girl who now stood trembling before
him; and the eagerness with which he listened to every
word can scarcely be imagined.

"Caution, however, was needed to insure success;
and the first question was how to dispose of the messenger so as to guard against arousing the suspicions
of the Arabs.

"With the instinct of the predatory chieftain, Gonzalez grasped his sword; but the murderous impulse
lasted only for a moment; for had not this innocent,
trembling girl been the means of his learning the secret
for the knowledge of which, one hour ago, he would
have freely given all he possessed? And yet she must
not be allowed to return to her people. For a few
minutes he was in perplexity how to dispose of her;
but at last a happy thought occurred to him. Untying
the sash which girded his waist, he bound the girl
hand and foot, promising not only to spare her life,
but to return her in safety to her kinsfolk ere many
hours had passed. Then, leaving her, he hastened to
the hamlet, where he communicated to his next in
command the discovery he had so unexpectedly made.
Two of his men were hurriedly despatched to the spot
where he had left the gipsy girl; while the rest of the
band, headed by Gonzalez, and accompanied by the
maniac and the young Arab prisoner, set out on the
road which led to the castle of Abdul Medshid.

" Since the Spaniards had become the masters of the land, Abdul Medshid had not been molested by them; for he regularly paid the tribute which they imposed upon every wealthy man, and gave food and wine to the lawless bands of plunderers who occasionally passed his castle.

" Melech-el-Hachem, who had been surprised and alarmed by this sudden breaking up of the camp at so untimely an hour of the night, regained his equanimity on being informed, by a sign from one of the Arabs, that the messenger would be sure to fulfil her errand.

" The band had now passed the ruins, and were close to the spot where Gonzalez had obtained the clue which he had so long and so vainly sought. Falling to the rear, he separated himself from the rest, and rode to the place where he had left the girl securely bound. As he no longer feared betrayal, he directed her to be released, and, giving her a handful of gold, bade her return in peace to her friends.

" Melech-el-Hachem did not for a moment doubt that his message had been safely carried to Abdul Medshid, and that the latter, made aware of the object of the expedition, would give a suitable reception to those who composed it, while he himself, freed by his people, should exchange places with his foe. Filled with these thoughts, and enjoying his anticipated triumph, the young Arab was no longer haughty and reserved : he even smiled and answered when addressed, as if reconciled to his fate.

" On Gonzalez this change in the demeanor of the prisoner produced an effect diametrically opposite from that which it had upon his men. For the first time, he began to think of the possibility of disappointment.

What if all that the midnight messenger had told him
were false,—a ruse to which the gipsy band had had
recourse in order to save the life of a superior of their
own creed and nation? Knowing the object of his
search, might they not have used her name as an un-
failing means of luring him into an ambuscade? As
he was pursuing this train of thought, he was accosted
by one of his men, who informed him that he had observed, while riding by the side of the maniac, that
incoherent words every now and then fell from the lips
of the latter, and that at each of these expressions the
Arab prisoner would indulge in a laugh.

"Gonzalez, who saw in this conduct of the Arab
a confirmation of the truth of the girl's story, bade the
man to watch and report to him, without fail, all that
might occur.

"The cavalcade had marched for many hours; and
the nearer they approached their destination the more
lively and communicative became the prisoner. At
last, emerging from a forest and coming out upon a
small plain, just as day was dawning, they beheld before them the residence of Abdul Medshid; and, as he
caught sight of it, the young Arab, throwing off all
restraint, shouted to the commander, 'Here it is at last!
Here you will find what you little expected!'

"He waved his white cashmere mantle in the air,
to indicate to his supposed rescuers his position in
the midst of the band, so that during the confusion of
attack he might not be taken for one of the enemy.
He pressed the sides of his charger in his excitement;
and the fiery animal seemed to share the emotions of
his rider, and pricked his ears, as if ready for the welcome that awaited them.

"The band continued to advance; and, when near enough to recognize and be recognized, Gonzalez gave a quick command to his men, who in an instant placed themselves in readiness for any emergency. No one in the palace, however, appeared to be aware of their coming; but the young Arab, believing that the inmates were feigning sleep and quietness, expected momently to hear the war-cry of 'Allah and Mohammed!' from his rescuing friends.

"But now, as they came close upon the palace, and silence still reigned, the prisoner's heart grew faint, the chilling doubt arose, 'Can it be that the messenger has not arrived?' and he resumed his former moody air, awaiting with anxiety the events which a few minutes must bring forth.

"Gonzalez now approached the prisoner, and, addressing him in a friendly tone, promised him life and wealth if he would divulge the secret of the whereabouts of the lost Estrella.

"The moment, however, was badly chosen: the bitter disappointment of the Arab, following so closely upon his hopes of deliverance and revenge, had made death a matter of indifference to him,—nay, even preferable to life; and he paid no attention to the words of his captor.

"Finding all his efforts useless, Gonzalez resolved to adopt other means. His first lieutenant was sent to the palace to summon Abdul Medshid before him. Ignorant of all that had transpired, the Moor soon appeared, accompanied by several of the officers of his household. With his accustomed courtesy, he desired to know the pleasure of his honored and welcome visitor. Then, with bowed head, he remained standing in the presence of Gonzalez, awaiting his commands.

"The answer of Gonzalez was short and decisive. He desired to be instantly led into the harem. Already, however, he had taken the necessary caution to prevent any hostile surprise; and, without waiting for the Moor's reply, he ordered him to lead the way. The tone and countenance of Gonzalez showed that remonstrances and entreaties would be without avail, and that nothing but instant compliance would avert harsh and violent measures; so, with a heavy sigh, Abdul Medshid prepared to obey the command of the detested foe.

"Passing through a long corridor, they entered an open space, or rotunda, lighted by a cupola of stained glass supported by thin marble columns of superb sculpture. Between each column were huge vases of exquisite material, in which grew exotic plants and vines, that twined around the pillars and covered them with rich festoons of variegated flowers, which looked as if made of wax, so symmetrically were they arranged between the glossy leaves.

"At the moment of the Spaniard's entrance, the rays of the sun, falling on the stained glass of the cupola, brought out in full effect the variegated colors, and gave to the whole interior the appearance of fairy-land. In the centre of the rotunda was a marble fountain of exquisite workmanship, the masterpiece of some Italian sculptor, from the centre of which a mermaid, supported by two sphynxes, threw the water in myriad jets into an elaborately carved basin, wherein disported hundreds of gold and silver fish of all species. The floor was covered with a rich carpet, into which the foot sank without sound. From the centre of the cupola depended, by a heavy ornamental chain, a massive silver vessel, from which distilled a vapor that penetrated to every corner of the rotunda, filling it with the most delicious perfume; while here and there were placed divans of elaborate workmanship, where one could recline and take in at a glance the entire wondrous scene.

"On any other occasion than the present, the magnificence of this rotunda, so suggestive of the immense wealth of its owner, would at once have roused in Gonzalez the rapacious thirst for gold which has always characterized the Spanish soldier; but so intently was he bent upon the all-absorbing object of ascertaining the fate of Estrella that the base passion remained dormant.

"This rotunda was the usual place of recreation for the inmates of the harem when prevented by the weather from enjoying the vast gardens of the palace; and passages led from it to the various private apartments of the women. To these apartments Gonzalez now requested to be led. Conducted by a eunuch, he entered the first apartment, having, as a measure of precaution, stationed a guard in the rotunda. The room to which he was led was small, but was fitted up in the style of uncalculating luxuriance for which the East has always been famed. The walls were hung with heavy drapery of a bluish tint, on which were embroidered, with golden thread, the figures of birds and flowers of the most graceful forms. All the surroundings exhibited a princely spirit on the part of the owner in contributing to the comfort and attending to the caprices of the occupant of the room; and the balmy odor that pervaded the apartment lent an air of enchantment to

the scene. In one corner was suspended a gigantic
sea-shell, in which reclined, on downy cushions and
wrapped in materials of the finest texture, a woman
of surpassing beauty. As the intruders approached,
the rattle of the Christian's sword startled the sylph-
like creature from her slumber. Raising herself on her
arm, she gazed at the unwonted spectacle in quiet
wonder; and her fair complexion and beautifully regular features showed that other climes than Africa had
contributed to the peopling of this earthly paradise.

"Gonzalez, though for a moment he could not with-
hold his admiration, was disappointed; for he did not
recognize in this fair being the one whom he sought.
In obedience to a sign from the Moor, the eunuch
led the way from the apartment, and conducted the
Spaniard to the next, and so on till they had visited
every room in the palace; but, alas! Estrella was not
to be found.

"Upon the return of the party to the rotunda, after
their fruitless search, a satisfied smile lit up the countenance of the Moor; while that of Gonzalez was expressive of the keenest disappointment. He now had
recourse to another expedient. Suddenly placing the
miniature in the medallion before the eyes of the com-
placent Abdul, he carefully watched the expression of
his face. The Moor, who recognized the features of
Estrella in those of the mother, could not conceal his
agitation: his face grew pale, and he bowed his head
as if to escape the penetrating glance of the Christian.
Gonzalez, seeing in these marks of emotion the evidence of a knowledge of the fate of Estrella, resolved
to make use of a further test. Summoning his lieutenant, he directed him, in a whisper, to bring in the

Arab prisoner. In a few moments Melech-el-Hachem made his appearance. The Moor, whose fears had been aroused by the mysterious movements of the two soldiers, glanced towards the entrance, and, recognizing at once the man who had brought to him by midnight the beautiful Spanish girl, he lost all self-possession, his countenance assumed an expression of dismay, and he staggered to one of the divans, upon which he threw himself, exclaiming, in a feeble voice, 'Allah is great, and Mohammed is his prophet!'

"This exclamation, in connection with the terror-stricken countenance and agitated frame of the Moor, proved conclusively to Gonzalez that Abdul Medshid had been concerned in the carrying away of La Estrella, either as principal or accessory. Ordering the Arab prisoner from his presence, he prepared to deal with the criminal.

"With bowed head and folded arms, Abdul Medshid stood before his stern judge, awaiting his fate. Supposing that the Spaniard knew all, and that dissimulation could serve him nothing, he was ready to make a full confession. He well knew what the result would be if he persisted in asserting his innocence of any part in the abduction: he had at first looked for nothing but the plundering of his treasures and the consigning of his castle to the flames; and now, making a virtue of necessity, he resolved to conceal nothing, in the hope that his only punishment would be the loss of Estrella.

"It cannot be denied that chance had singularly favored Gonzalez in his search. The capture of Melech-el-Hachem, the discovery of the medallion, and the midnight meeting with the gipsy girl, had all been

the result of accident rather than of his own efforts.
Seeing himself now so near the object of his wishes, he
readily accepted the Moor's offer to confess, promising
that, if he withheld nothing of the truth, he would
spare his life and property.

"Abdul, encouraged by this promise, kept back
nothing, and promised to restore Estrella to liberty
and deliver her into the chieftain's hands before sunset; but her present whereabouts he positively refused
to disclose. Once more the suspicions of Gonzalez were
aroused: he dared not trust the infidel out of his sight,
and he feared that his only object was to gain time.
As, in view of Abdul's high standing and consequent
influence, a few hours' delay might have been fatal to
the success of the enterprise, he insisted on an immediate restoration, threatening the direst penalties if he
were not instantly obeyed.

"The Moor was now sadly perplexed. He knew
that Gonzalez would not suffer him out of his sight for
a moment; and to conduct him to the abode of Estrella
was to divulge a secret dearer, almost, than life itself.
He reasoned, supplicated, and even offered to forfeit
his castle with all its treasures should he fail to keep
his word. The Spaniard, however, was inflexible:
long experience during his predatory excursions had
taught him to be firm in his resolutions. He refused
to listen to the Moor's reasonings and prayers; and,
the pertinacity of the infidel at last rousing his ire, he
drew his sword with a menacing gesture and darkened
brow.

"Abdul Medshid clung to life, his women, and his
gold with all the tenacity of the debauchee and the
miser; and, aware of the utter indifference with which

the Christian murdered the infidel, he proceeded forthwith to carry out the commands of Gonzalez, begging only that he would follow him alone.

"Gonzalez, though a brave man, still would not trust the Moor. An open enemy had no terrors for him, but he dreaded treachery: he therefore ordered his men to accompany him within easy hailing distance. Abdul Medshid, seeing now that there was no alternative, led the way, accompanied by the Spanish chieftain, while the men, with the maniac and the Arab prisoner in their midst, followed at a short distance.

"As you are aware, there were two ways of entering the subterranean harem; and, to preserve the secret of the hollowed tree, the Moor concluded to make use of the walled-up door, and immediately ordered it to be broken away. Gonzalez gazed on this operation with feelings of amazement and disappointment: there was nothing outside to indicate the abode of the living; and, when he witnessed the demolition of the door, what wonder that he should suppose it to be the entrance to a sepulchre, in which lay buried the mortal remains of her whom he had so long and eagerly sought? And now the thought suddenly occurred to him that the Moor, in promising to return the abducted girl, had not said whether she should be delivered alive or dead. Now he saw all clearly: Estrella was no more; and all that would be returned to him was her corpse.

"Infuriated by the thought, he drew his sword, and, with a cry like that of a savage beast, rushed upon the Moor. The latter, ignorant of the cause of this sudden outbreak, and fearing that he had disclosed more of his secret than it had been his intention to do, darted at once into the entrance, followed closely by the Spaniard.

"The furious cry of Gonzalez, and his disappearance, sword in hand, into the entrance, soon brought his men to the spot. Seeing the open door, they unhesitatingly entered it, abandoning, in their excitement and bewilderment, both the maniac and the Arab prisoner.

"But a few moments had elapsed when the sound of a terrible explosion rent the air: a thick dark smoke obscured the sun, and huge stones and trees were thrown upward and scattered on every side, as if nature herself were convulsed: a sulphurous vapor filled the air, and destruction reigned supreme.

"Some days later, a party of nomads who had chanced to pass this way were actively engaged among the ruins in search of gold and other valuables which were scattered around, and, while thus occupied, met with two disfigured human bodies lying side by side. One had the feet and hands loaded with shackles, and from all appearance was that of an Arab; the other was poorly clad, and, as far as they could judge from the features and dress, was the body of what they styled a 'Christian dog.'

"The eminence under which the harem had been excavated had fallen in, leaving a hollow space, over which were scattered the marble slabs that had been used in the construction of the palace. It is supposed that Abdul Medshid, fearing treachery on the part of his foe, and choosing to involve all in one common death rather than suffer the hated Spaniard to despoil him of his treasures, had fired some hidden store of explosives, and thus at one blow destroyed the harem, with its beauteous inmates, himself, and his enemies.

"Not long after the events which I have narrated, some kind Christian, impressed by the sad fate of the young Spanish maiden, planted a cross here, and named the spot La Estrella del Moro."

As Mademoiselle Hortense finished her story, I looked at my watch, and was astonished to find that it was past six o'clock. So interested had I been in her recital that I had altogether forgotten my appointment to meet the fisherman at four o'clock in order to accompany him to the coral-fishery. As the sun had not yet set, we concluded to visit the spot so closely connected with the mournful tradition which she had so eloquently narrated for my entertainment. On our arrival, we found the place exactly as she had described it. There was the eminence, and in its centre an irregular hollow, and, although more than two hundred years had elapsed since the destruction of the subterranean palace, pieces of marble were still to be seen scattered here and there. A few of the smallest of these fragments I picked up and brought with me, as remembrancers of the sad episode with which I had been made acquainted; and these I still preserve among my curiosities of travel. Not far from the hollow which has been described, a dilapidated passage-way is still to be seen; and this, probably, was one of the means of communication with the under-ground harem.

Some twelve years after I heard the above story, and at the time when the convents of the monks in Mexico were destroyed by order of the so-called Liberal government, I chanced to find, among the books of the library of the convent of San Domingo, a worm-eaten manuscript, purporting to be a translation from the French of the Benedictine monk Augustin Calmet, of the congregation of St. Vito. In this manuscript mention is made of the above history of La Estrella del Moro. Calmet was born in the village of Mesnil-la-Horgue, in Lorraine, on the 26th of February, 1672. At the early age of sixteen he became a Benedictine monk. In the convent of his order he found a grammar of the Semitic languages, by Buxtorf; and, having become acquainted with the Arabic tongue, he desired to be sent as a missionary to the East. In 1692 he visited the spot where occurred the events narrated in the preceding pages. In one of his unpublished manuscripts mention is made of the above tradition; and, as he was the author of many meritorious works published at Leipsic between 1704 and 1720, I could not help giving some credence to the story, naturally allowing some latitude for its embellishments as told by a charming young lady of vivid imagination and romantic disposition.

The same evening, after our return to the settlement of Bastion de France, I took copious notes of the narrative, which have served me in its reproduction on these pages.

On the following day I went to see the fisherman with whom I had made the appointment for the preceding afternoon. I was just in time; for he and his companions were ready to set out on their expedition. I had only a few moments in which to change my clothes for the outfit which the fisherman had provided for me. It consisted of rough sackcloth painted with oil, and a hat of the same material, similar to those worn by sailors in rough weather. Thus prepared,

I took my seat in the boat, making the fifth occupant. We immediately set out for the reefs, which are some twelve miles from the shore; and, to beguile the tedium of the voyage, I began to examine the instruments which the fishermen use in gathering the coral. I had by this time acquired some knowledge of the Arab language, and, although far from being able to converse freely, could manage to make myself understood.

I had found, in my travels through Asia Minor, Egypt, and Europe, that more information can be obtained from the common people in relation to local traditions than from the upper class of society; and, whenever opportunity presented, I endeavored to ingratiate myself with the sailor, the peasant, the shepherd, or the laborer. In my boyhood's days I used to drink in with avidity the stories related to me by the Hungarian shepherds,—stories based on historical facts, yet which, on searching for them in after-years, I failed to find mentioned by any of the so-called national authors.

Along the Danube, from the ruins of Theben, near Presburg, down to the Dardanelles, I learned more from the peasantry than could be derived from any book ever written by any national author. The peasant is familiar with every spot in his vicinity. He can tell you at once where a certain battle with the Turks was fought, or where some other incident of historical note occurred. If there is an old ruin in the neighborhood, he knows all the legends connected with it, which have been handed down to him by oral tradition; and if his language is not poetical, it has at least the charm of truth. In fifteen minutes he will tell you more facts than you could obtain in as many hours from reading

the book of a historical novelist; for, though he knows
nothing of romance or of embellishment, and fancy is a
stranger to him, yet the most graphic pen, in describing
the scene of a great historical incident, would sink into
dulness beside the peasant's homely narrative told by
word of mouth. The author of the historical romance
speaks to you, in all probability, of many places which
he has never seen, and the field of his operations is a
very extended one; but the peasant describes what he
personally knows; he is familiar with it, he lives in
its sphere, and paints with the true colors of nature.

All the information I have obtained in my travels
relative to local traditions, &c. came, with very rare exceptions, from the class of people of whom I have just
spoken; and whenever I have occasion to make use of
the knowledge thus acquired, I endeavor to reproduce,
as far as possible, the very words of the narrator, con-
fining myself to facts, and leaving the embellishments
of language to those who, endowed with the gift of
fancy, can make a volume or two out of a story that
might be told in half a dozen pages. As an illustration, I will relate what occurred to me in the year
1846, when on a pedestrian excursion in the Carpathian Mountains, in company with a young Prussian
noble who had some inclination for literature. Baron
C—— was of an adventurous disposition: he travelled
for pleasure, had his valet with him, and was provided
with all the requisites for bodily comfort. Sometimes,
as we passed some purling brook, I would use my hat
as a drinking-cup; but the pure and cooling beverage
would be handed to him by his valet in a silver goblet
bearing the family crest. When fatigued, and resolved
to rest, I composed myself to sleep on nature's beautiful

carpet, while for him a heavy cloth was spread by the valet; and yet, I doubt not, my slumbers were as undisturbed and as refreshing as his. I did not envy him in the least his appliances of luxury: nay, to me they would have been an annoyance rather than a comfort.

We visited in company one of the wildest and most romantic spots on the globe.

The English, who have made themselves famous as travellers, especially within the present century, do not seem to have thought of visiting this region, which certainly, for its wild and sublime scenery, deserves more notice than it has ever received.

The place to which I allude is in the "Liptauen Comitat," in the Carpathian Mountains. Page after page has been filled with accounts of the doings of Attila, and other heroes of the Huns; but very little is known of the men who, a thousand years ago, built on the highest peaks of those mountains the stately castles whose ruins still withstand the ravages of time and impress the thoughtful traveller by their majestic proportions.

The Carpathian Mountains form here a chain that separates Hungary from Galicia, and numerous ruins are hidden among the thick forests. Could these ruins speak, they would tell many a tale of fierce conflict, many a romantic incident in the life of fair damsel or brave knight-errant.

The inhabitants of this region are wretchedly poor: the greater part of them pass through life without ever tasting any thing else than black bread, sheep's cheese, beans, meat at rare intervals, and occasionally a drop of whiskey. Their clothes consist of a rough piece of sackcloth, which before it is put on is smeared with fat, and then is worn until it falls from the body in rags. During the winter, which lasts nearly eight months, they use a sheepskin as a garment. Only the better class wear covering for the feet, in the form of a piece of leather shaped like a sandal, the rest going barefoot.

Their only means of subsistence is the cutting of wood in the summer for contractors. This wood is rafted down the Waag, entering the Danube at Comorn, whence it is conveyed to Pesth.

Their houses, consisting of one apartment, are con-structed of the rough trunks of trees, and plastered in-side with mud or clay. Sometimes one house is in-habited by eight or ten families, together with a few pigs, and, among the better class, a cow or two.

In the centre of this family residence, a hole is made in the earth, which serves as a fireplace or kitchen range; while at the side or ends sheepskins are laid on the ground, and take the place of the civilized bedstead.

Over the fireplace in the centre is found the most useful piece of furniture. It consists of an iron kettle supported by stones (bricks, so far as my observation extended, are unknown in this region). In this kettle all their cooking is done, and from it, as soon as the meal is prepared, the members of the family, gathering around, partake with wooden spoons of home manu-facture. Knives and forks are never seen; in fact, there is ordinarily no occasion for them; and if any sick animal be condemned to die, in the resulting feast the flesh that falls to the lot of each one is conveyed to the mouth by means of the implements which nature has provided. Their usual meal consists of kasha,—a kind of buckwheat, the grain of which is cooked, without any preparation by crushing or grinding, until it forms a paste, which is rendered savory by the addition of a little salt.

This kasha is grown on cleared spaces in the woods, but by no means in abundance; for the poverty of the people is so great that during the summer the male portion of the adult population emigrate in search of labor, bringing their earnings home for the support of their families during the winter.

When I said, above, that the only means of subsistence of this people is wood-cutting, I had forgotten another source of profit, and one of considerable importance to these wretched creatures. It is a harvest which is gathered twice a year, but belongs entirely to the fairer portion of the population.

Twice in the year these miserable beings, scattered here and there throughout the mountains, are visited by pedlars, who come provided with trinkets, such as glass corals, brass ear-rings, colored neckkerchiefs, and other imitations of those articles of luxury so generally coveted by the fair daughters of Eve, no matter in what part of the globe they reside.

The arrival of one of these pedlars is the signal for a general outburst of joy. As soon as he has taken up his abode, the women assemble from all quarters, bringing as their sole marketable commodity that which nature has made one of the principal elements of female beauty,—their hair.

On this article the women of that part of the country bestow great care; indeed, it may be said to monopolize the attention due to other parts of the person. They will sometimes comb it for hours, with wooden combs made by themselves; but seldom, if ever, do they wash their faces or necks; and I have seen some of them so filthy that the dirt was encrusted upon the skin in scales. The men look a little cleaner than the women; but I suppose that is merely on account of their more frequent contact with the outside world; and certainly neither sex could pass muster in any civilized community.

The hair of these women is, beyond all question, extremely beautiful. It is fine, silky, and glossy; and in all my travels I have never seen it surpassed, except perhaps among the Indians of Tehuantepec: it attains the length of thirty-six to forty inches.

As soon as a certain number of women who have brought their hair for sale have congregated, the pedlar, who generally comes from the capital of Hungary or of Austria, inspects the wares, and passes his judgment as to quality, quantity, and length. Now commences the trade. The highest price paid for a superior quality of hair is eight *golden* (or, at the time of my visit, one dollar and eighty cents in American money); while the lowest price averages from two to three florins.

The price agreed upon, the tonsorial operation begins. The pedlar skilfully wields his large, keen scissors, taking care to cut as close as possible, and soon all his victims have passed under the steel.

If these creatures look hideous with the only ornament they possess, it will readily be credited that the loss of their hair does not improve their appearance. I verily believe their own lords and masters find it a matter of difficulty to recognize them upon their return to the domestic fireside.

After the hair has been all cut off, the next business in order is payment; and now the pedlar, with an eye to trade, and aware of the luxurious extravagance of the female sex, artfully displays his tempting merchandise, which is almost devoured by the covetous glances of his customers. Glass imitations of coral, brass earrings of immense size, colored rosaries, and sometimes even candies, are offered in lieu of money; and many are the disappointments of those who are prevented from indulging their fancies to the full by the necessity of taking home some cash to their liege lords, who claim a share in the spoil.

The day of hair-selling, as I have remarked above, is considered a special feast. It is one of the few days in the year when *korznalka*, or whiskey, commands a high price in the market; and it is the one also, of all others, on which the husband and father presses to his heart, with grateful affection, the wife and daughter, blessing Providence for the possession of so certain a source of profit.

In the whole of this district there is probably not one in a hundred who knows how to read and write. The male population is divided into two classes. One of these, called "Drathbinder," wander through the country the whole year round, selling wire mousetraps, and mending broken kitchen-utensils; the other emigrate during a part of the year, and engage in lumbering, or, when the grape-harvest begins, find employment in the vineyards of Lower Hungary. They are usually away from home about four months, and spend their earnings during the winter in the bosom of their families.

To this region of the Carpathians I and my Teutonic
8*

companion went in company; but after the lapse of a single day my aristocratic friend became so utterly disgusted that he lost all taste for that class of adventure, and declared his determination to get back at once to more cultivated society. Being myself of a democratic turn of mind, I concluded to stay, promising to join him in a short time at a place called Biala, in Silesia. I remained for more than three weeks in this region, visiting a fresh locality every day, partaking heartily of the kasha, and sleeping as comfortably as circumstances would allow, on a filthy sheepskin, in company with hogs, cows, and the dirtier human animals.

I could fill a volume with the experience of those three weeks. Many an interesting story did I hear while sitting with the others around the rude fireplace, and many a song in praise of the brave deeds of their heroes; for, like their more civilized brethren, these semi-barbarians have had their Homers, and the songs of their forefathers have been handed down to the present by oral tradition.

Bidding farewell, at last, to these wild children of nature, I rejoined my aristocratic Prussian friend. I found him installed in one of the first hotels of the place, intently occupied in arranging his notes of travel. He begged me to relate my adventures among the inhabitants of the Carpathians, which of course I did willingly. Some years afterwards, happening to meet with a book published in Breslau by Baron C——, entitled "Adventures in the Carpathian Mountains," I was astonished to find in it all that I had told him concerning my experiences among the Slovacks, &c., himself figuring as the *bona fide* traveller who had

seen and heard all these strange things. I entertained
no feeling of harshness towards him, however; for his
style was so pleasing, and he represented himself as
such a hero, that I could not help being entertained
and amused. Occasionally he fell into gross exaggera-
tion; as, for instance, when he said that, obliged to
seek shelter in one of the Slovack dwellings, the sheepskin which the inmates furnished him to sleep on was
so filled with vermin that both bed and sleeper were
transported during the night to a considerable distance,
and he found himself next morning several yards away
from the habitation.

The whole work was, in fact, little better than an
improved version of Baron Munchausen, although it
was mainly based on the stories related to me by the
people of the Carpathians, but with the facts distorted
out of all semblance to truth. Nevertheless, it gained
admittance to many respectable libraries as a reliable
and valuable work.

And now to return to my coral-fishing, from which
I have wandered considerably while endeavoring to
make good the assertion that I have always found that
the most minute local information, in whatever part of
the world, is to be had from the lower classes. I had
been but a short time in the boat with the Arab fishermen, when, acting on this conviction, I commenced to
make myself acquainted with the men, hoping to draw
out some story or legend during our sail to the reefs.

My four companions were Kabyls, the oldest of
whom occupied the position of sheik, or chief of the
natives who live within his jurisdiction. Among the
Kabyls who have not been subdued by the French, the
sheik is at once priest, legislator, and judge. And

here I must be permitted to correct an error into
which many have fallen,—myself, for a time, among
the number.

The Kabyl, or Berber, is often denominated an Arab,
or Moor; but there is a great difference between the
two races. The Kabyls are supposed to have been the
aboriginal inhabitants; and they now live in regular
villages in the mountainous region which lies towards
the desert of Sahara.

The domestic duties of the household are intrusted
exclusively to the women, while the men occupy themselves in hunting. Those who live at some distance
from the French possessions are, as a rule, robbers, and
exceedingly cruel and treacherous : yet the most civilized people of Europe will not show a stranger such
warm hospitality as he will find among the Kabyls.
Once obtain the friendship of a Kabyl, and you may
rest assured that no harm will befall you which he can
avert. But, while they are so kind to their guests,
anticipating, if possible, every wish, the savage Indian
of America is not so cruel as the Kabyl towards those
whom he considers his enemies. Once, in conversing
with a half-civilized Kabyl, I took occasion to speak
of these contradictory traits in their character,—when
he assured me that they are not naturally cruel, but have
only become so since the incursion of the foreigners.

The Kabyl has an inborn antipathy to all kinds of
trade. He is either a hunter or a shepherd,—those of
the latter calling preferring to live in caves. Like the
Indians of North America, they are very proud of their
claim to be the original inhabitants of the country; and
they stigmatize as bastards the Moors, Arabs, Turks,
and Koloughs.

Their religion, except in the case of a very few, is Islamism, and their language a corrupt Arabic. They dislike all foreigners, but especially hate the French; and my German friend at Algiers, the bookkeeper of Oser ben Levi, warned me, when I left that city, that if ever I came in contact with a Kabyl the first thing I should do would be to let him know I was not a Frenchman. He will not, it is true, overwhelm with kindness the European who belongs to any other nation; but he will not regard him with the feeling of fierce hatred which he entertains towards the French invader.

It may from this be readily inferred that my conversation with the fishermen opened by letting them know that I was not one of the detested nation; but I was surprised to find that the announcement did not make the slightest impression upon them. I had expected to hear at least the customary invocation of Allah and his prophet; but, instead of their manifesting even that degree of enthusiasm, it appeared to me that their reserve increased, if that were indeed possible.

The Kabyl whose lot is cast among Europeans never speaks to those not of his own race, except in answer to a question, and even then he wastes no words; his brethren of the mountains, on the contrary, are exceedingly communicative, and one of them will entertain the traveller for an hour at a time with a story which might without difficulty be condensed into five minutes.

Finding the crew so little disposed to enter into conversation, I looked forward to an exceedingly monotonous voyage, and was almost ready to regret that I had undertaken the journey. I soon felt myself becoming drowsy; but I struggled with all my might against the temptation to sleep, since I could not get rid of an ill-

defined foreboding of sinister designs against me on
the part of my taciturn and surly companions.

After proceeding in silence for a considerable time,
however, the men made some advances towards entering into conversation. My drooping spirits revived at
this unexpected change; but soon a question was put
to me which caused me heartily to repent the curiosity
that had prompted me to visit the coral-fishery. My
interrogator desired to know how much money I had
brought with me. Did I understand him aright? Did
it depend on my answer whether I was worth murdering and throwing overboard or not? I confess, I knew
not, for a few moments, how to frame a reply; but,
collecting my thoughts as rapidly as circumstances
would permit, I thrust my hand in my pocket and
drew therefrom a handful of silver coin, which I begged
them to accept, promising to give them twice as much
on our safe return to port.

Hardly had I finished my stammering reply, couched
in the broken Arabic which was the best at my command, when the entire party burst into a hearty laugh,
at the same time making the most emphatic negative
motions with their heads. Taking this to mean that
I had not been sufficiently liberal, I assured them that
I had no more money with me, and, in my eagerness
to prove the truth of what I said, began to turn my
pockets inside out, earnestly reiterating my promise to
reward them munificently when they should have safely
landed me at Bona once more. At that moment the
old leader, who commenced to understand the mistake
I had made, stepped up to me, and, taking me by the
hand, explained, in the most reassuring tones he could
command, that I had entirely misapprehended the drift

of the question that had so alarmed me. It seems that the impression on the part of all on board, with the exception of the old sheik, had been that I was a coral-merchant, accompanying the crew with the intention of purchasing on the spot whatever they might find, it being quite customary with these fishermen thus to sell at a hazard the fruit of an evening's labor. Hence their desire to know how much money I had brought with me.

After this explanation I breathed more freely, begging the men to pardon me for having attributed to them the design of robbing and murdering me; and, as I compared the real motive of the alarming question with the one that I had conjectured for it, I could not do otherwise than join in the general laughter.

This incident, which in the beginning had assumed to me so serious an aspect, was the means of effecting a perfect understanding between myself and the fishermen. The ice once broken, the reserve of the Kabyls soon melted away entirely; and the conversation did not flag for a moment until we arrived in the immediate neighborhood of the reefs. The time had passed much more pleasantly than I anticipated at the outset; and, altogether, I had every reason to be delighted, for it is not often that a traveller falls in with a party of friendly Kabyls.

Feeling now perfectly at ease, I began to look around me, and was soon asking questions with all the pertinacity of a Down-Easter, and examining every article in the boat that was new to me. One of the first objects that attracted my attention was the matting which had been spread for me to sit upon. I had seen the same kind of matting before, at various places, during

my wanderings; but it had always happened that other
things had so engrossed my attention as to leave me no
opportunity of satisfying my curiosity respecting its
manufacture. I ascertained from my friends the fishermen that it is made from the leaf of the dwarf palm,
one of the most useful and abundant vegetable productions of the country. Baskets of exquisite finish are
made from these leaves, and exported to France, meeting there with a ready sale. From the same material
are manufactured ropes, cord, bags, matting, and a kind
of netting resembling that used for hammocks; while
the tender footstalks and young flowers afford a nutri-
tious and palatable food, which is highly prized by the
natives. At the base of the Little Atlas, which termi-
nates west of Bona, the dwarf palm grows in abundance, and furnishes to many of the Arabs their sole
means of subsistence.

My curiosity on this point satisfied, I turned my
attention to the implements used in the fisheries. The
tools used by the coral-fishers of Bona differ considerably from any that I ever saw elsewhere. The principal instrument consists of two long spars or poles,
fastened together, about twelve inches from one end,
by a movable screw. It looks like a huge pair of scissors, and can be opened and shut with great facility.
To the end of each of the longer arms is attached a
contrivance in the shape of a lobster's opened claw,
which serves, when the apparatus is submerged, to break
off the coral from the rocks. The next instrument in
importance is a pole somewhat longer than the spars
of the other, which is furnished at one end with a wire
basket: this is used to secure the coral after it has been
broken off by the first-mentioned instrument.

The coral-fisheries at Bona are by no means so productive as I had supposed. My companions informed me that they were out sometimes for thirty or forty hours, and the value of their catch would not be more than five francs. The oldest fisherman on board told me that the largest amount of coral he had ever gathered in any single excursion did not exceed in value forty francs,—about eight dollars. This was an unexpected and dampening piece of information to me; for my impression had been that I should be able to gather with my own hands a couple of bagfuls at least.

Towards six o'clock we arrived at the first reefs. Here the boat was made fast to a rock, and the men prepared to enter upon their labors, urging me to follow their example,—that is, doff my nether garment and wade through the water to the adjacent reef.

It is a pleasing task to describe past adventures, seated in a cosy little library, in front of a cheerful fire and with all sources of annoyance banished, bringing back the scenes in which you took part long ago, and jotting down your remembrances for the entertainment of others; but the participation in the adventures themselves is often quite another matter. At the coral-fishing grounds, for instance, instead of your feet being encased in Turkish slippers, you are obliged to wade barefoot through the water over the reefs,—a decidedly unpleasant experience, particularly to one unaccustomed to that species of pedestrianism over stones whose surface is not remarkable for polish and which are not laid with the regularity that characterizes the work of the mason. Then, again, in lieu of the easy-fitting, luxurious *robe-de-chambre* in which you are wrapped while describing your adventure, you have an uncouth suit of oiled sackcloth, not wonderful for cleanliness, and which proves of very little service when you are in the water. It is the difference between practice and theory, between the past and the present.

Upon seeing the fishermen, up to the waist in water, picking their way cautiously and laboriously over the slippery rocks, I concluded that coral-fishing did not altogether accord with my tastes, and declined the pleasure of accompanying the party, preferring to remain in the boat and watch the operation from a distance. After many vain attempts to induce me to follow them, the men set off, wishing me at the same time a pleasant *tob-lail*, or good-night.

"Surely," thought I, "they do not intend to leave me here the whole night, alone in the boat, without any one near me on whom to call in case of emergency." For the second time I began to repent having come on the excursion, and would gladly have paid fifty francs to be at once taken back to the settlement. But it was too late for that now: the men were already beyond hailing-distance, and I must make up my mind to pass the night with nothing but my thoughts for company. It was not the prospect of being alone until the morning that troubled me, so much as the apprehension that some other party of fishermen might chance to pass that way, and, finding me asleep and companionless, rob and murder me. But one other course was now open to me; and I immediately resolved to take that. Hurriedly divesting myself of my trousers, I plunged into the water, and followed in the wake of my companions as rapidly as possible, though not without several vexatious falls on the slippery rocks, until I caught up with them. Carefully concealing the real cause of my altered resolution, I told them I had found it impossible to resist the impulse of curiosity to witness their operations; and, gratified at my interest in their perilous occupation, they extended to me a most hearty welcome.

I shall now give a brief description of the substance called coral, and of the manner in which it is gathered.

The red coral of commerce (*Corallium rubrum*) is the production of a marine animal, but so closely resembles in form certain species of plants that until recently it was considered as belonging to the vegetable kingdom. The cells composing the coral are the habitation of the animal, and are so built upon each other as to produce a branched, tree-like structure, very beautiful in form and color, and exceedingly hard. Coral was known to the ancients, who, however, erroneously supposed it to be soft while in the water, and to become hard only when brought into the air or in contact with the hand. It is found in various parts of the Mediterranean, the Red Sea, and the Persian Gulf; but the principal source is the Mediterranean. It grows in waters of the depth of from three hundred to six hundred feet, and is almost invariably found either in submarine caves or on shelving rocks. In the former localities it is much larger, more abundant, and of greater value than in the latter. Its ordinary growth is about twelve inches, and after a branch has been broken off an interval of ten or twelve years is required to bring it again to perfection. It does not appear, however, that it will attain any greater height than twelve inches, no matter how long it be allowed to remain undisturbed. In consequence of this peculiarity in its growth, the fishing-grounds are divided into ten sections, from each of

which the coral is removed only once in ten years.
The implements of the fishermen I have already described. The extremities of the two crossed spars are
wrapped around with loosely-twisted hemp and coarse
netting, and, being sunk by means of heavy stones
attached to the middle, the instrument is guided by
ropes into the places where the coral is most abundant.
The branching form of the coral causes it to become
entangled in the hemp and network, by which means
it is broken off from the rock. The pole with the wire
basket attached to the end serves to catch the pieces
that are not retained by the netting. The uses of coral
are known to all, and require no mention here.

Towards five in the morning we returned to Bona ;
and, looking back upon the adventure, I felt very well
satisfied with the results, in spite of its disagreeable
incidents. The information I had acquired was well
worth all the trouble I had undergone and all the
anxieties I had experienced.

When I arrived at Bastion de France, I delivered
into the hands of La Belle Hortense, as I had promised
before setting out, the coral which I had taken,—by no
means an overwhelming quantity,—and in the conversation that ensued was astonished to find that not one of
the family had ever had curiosity enough to visit the
fisheries, although Lasalle himself was in the habit of
buying from the fishermen for export to France. Their
very proximity seemed to have destroyed all curiosity
concerning what to a traveller would have been an object of great interest. This indifference to local nota-
bilities is not confined to Algeria, however, as the
reader is doubtless aware for himself. I well remember
how, when I landed in the United States, one of the

first things I did was to visit the capital, and before many days had passed I knew every public building and had seen all that was worth seeing in Washington. Some years afterwards, I became acquainted with a wealthy merchant of Baltimore, a man twenty-four years of age; and, an allusion being made to the city of Washington during one of our conversations, I found that he had never been there, which astonished me even more than did the want of curiosity on the part of the Lasalles concerning the coral-fishing.

On the afternoon of the day on which I returned from the fishery I took leave of my kind host and his beautiful kinswoman, whose charms both of person and mind had made an impression upon me that required the lapse of many months of exciting adventure to weaken it; and even now I can recall the image of La Belle Hortense, and look back with pleasure to the many hours spent in her company.

Upon my return to Bona I met a party of Frenchmen who were going to Oran, and at once determined to accompany them. I might have taken a more direct route to Tlemcen, but the temptation of journeying in the company of civilized men was too great to be overcome by any considerations of time or distance.

Oran is the capital and principal city of the province of the same name, distant from Algiers about two hundred miles, and pleasantly situated on the shore of the Mediterranean. It has the appearance of a Spanish South-American city, except where the general effect is broken by the more recently-built houses, erected by the various foreigners who have established themselves here since the French occupation. Of the twenty-five thousand inhabitants, about two-thirds are Europeans;

9*

and, like Algiers, Oran is rapidly losing the Moorish character and becoming to all intents a French city. The older buildings are all of Spanish construction; for the province was a dependency of the crown of Castile for three centuries, and did not revert to its original owners until the year 1792. The principal building in the place, though now in a very ruinous condition, is the one that was occupied as a palace by the Turkish Dey, Pasha, or military governor before the French took possession of the country in 1830.

The province, of course, is under French authority, and justice is dispensed to Europeans by French tribunals; but for the Jews courts are held presided over by Rabbis, or Shofet, and for the natives the judge is a cadi. The operation of this system is by no means advantageous to other than French litigants; for if a Jew have a complaint to prefer against a native, he must go to the cadi; while if it be a native against a Jew, the former must have recourse to the rabbi; and since—as might be expected—they never agree, the disputants are compelled to appeal to the French court, where, as a rule, strict and impartial justice is meted out. In the native courts no case can be finally adjudged except one between two natives; and in the Jewish courts the same restriction applies to all suits except those between Jews.

While in Oran I had the good fortune to be present at the trial of a very remarkable case in a Jewish court. It involved the rights of Arab, Jew, and Christian as affected by the laws of marriage and inheritance; and when it is borne in mind that the result of the trial depended in a great degree on the customs of the various sects to which the parties belonged, it will not be hard to believe that the case excited the most intense interest among the entire population, foreign no less than native. Such, indeed, was its importance that the French governor had directed a mixed court to be formed, consisting of a cadi, a rabbi, and a French judge, that there might be no opportunity for the dissatisfied to suspect injustice or bias on the part of the tribunal. As the case was of so extraordinary a nature, and promised many interesting developments of the native character and customs, I at once resolved to be present at the trial until its conclusion, and to take copious notes of the proceedings. These notes I here reproduce, in the belief that they will not fail to excite the interest of the reader.

In the interior of the province of Oran is a small town called El-Callah, of some importance by reason of the trade it carries on with Fez and Morocco. At the time of the events which gave rise to the trial I am about to describe, the principal man and wealthiest inhabitant of this town was an Arab of high rank, by name Musta-el-Geber. For many years he carried on an extensive caravan trade, and, besides, was the proprietor of the rich lead-mines of Jebel Wanashrees and Mascara, the ore from which yields from seventy-five to eighty per cent. of the pure metal. The Wanashrees is the loftiest peak of the Atlas chain in the province of Oran, and, like the Jurjura, southeast of Algiers, is crowned with snow throughout the year. The possession of mines like these could not fail to add largely to the wealth of Musta-el-Geber; and the extent of his trade with the oases and with Fez and Morocco may be imagined from the fact that he constantly had about fifteen hundred camels employed in transportation.

Some years after the French became possessed of the country he sold out his interest to two brothers, Jews, and retired to private life. The new proprietors of the lead-mines resided at Mascara, another interior town of Oran, where they had acquired immense wealth, and, previous to the purchase from Musta-el-Geber, had been his partners in many of his heaviest commercial undertakings.

The old merchant was always looked upon by the natives, Jews as well as Arabs, as the protector and patron of the two Jewish brothers, who seemed to sustain towards him the relation of intimate friends, differing from him only in the matter of religious belief, rather than that of partners in trade, connected for the mere sake of pecuniary advantage.

Like all other Arabs of high rank, Musta had his harem; and his wealth enabled him to fill it with the choicest flowers of the slave-market. Among the fairest of these was one whom he preferred above all the others, and who occupied the position of "Sultana," as the favorite wife is called among the higher class of Arabs. Whence she came, and how he obtained her, however, nobody could tell. All that was certainly known of her was that she had arrived in company with him some twenty years back, on his return from a commercial expedition with one of his caravans from Morocco, and that her name was Marhara.

After the French invasion, our merchant did not hold aloof from the infidel conquerors, but, on the contrary, seemed to prefer their company and to admire their institutions. His residence was open to the visits of the Europeans, and he mingled with them as freely as though they had been of his own nationality and religion. Nor was Marhara kept in the seclusion so customary with the Arab women: she was introduced to his visitors, and became known to them all as his wife, or, as the French generally called her, Madame Musta. A beautiful and intelligent woman, and speaking French with extraordinary fluency, her society was eagerly sought by the better class of the foreign population of El-Callah.

Marhara was the mother of one child, whose birth Musta had caused to be registered in the French court, and whom, as soon as she arrived at a suitable age, he had sent to one of the best Christian schools in the country, at which she remained until the completion of her fifteenth year.

When Marhara first came to El-Callah, her appearance had given rise to a multitude of conjectures and rumors concerning her nationality. Some insisted that she was a Christian, born of French parents in Morocco; others would have it that she was the daughter of an indigent Jew of Fez, from whom Musta had obtained her at an enormous price. All this, of course, was mere surmise; and, as time passed on, the gossips, finding nothing on which to base their structures, ceased to speak or even to think about the mysterious stranger.

When the daughter of Musta was brought back to her home, after the completion of her education, the little world of El-Callah once more became a field for the operations of Dame Rumor. It was now noised abroad that the young and beautiful heiress of the wealthy merchant was to be married to the younger of the two brothers who had recently purchased his business interest and his share of the Wanashrees and

Mascara lead-mines.   The announcement occasioned
no little excitement, on account of the girl's father
being a Mohammedan, while the bridegroom was a
Jew. What arrangements were entered into between
the two was known to no one: suffice it to say that the
fair Elila, the daughter of Musta-el-Geber and his
favorite Marhara, was married publicly to Henoch ben
Ezocher in the Jewish synagogue, in conformity with
the rites of her husband's religion and under the sanction of the French civil judge.

The gossips being now thoroughly on the alert, the
vexed question of the ancestry of Marhara, the bride's
mother, was once more agitated.   This time, however,
there was less division of opinion than on the former
occasion; for now it was generally conceded that she
must be a Jewess, since not only had she given her
consent to the marriage of her daughter to a Jew, but
had apparently been the principal agent in bringing
it about.   This point settled to everybody's satisfaction,
the whole matter was soon forgotten, and the scandal-
mongers and busybodies turned their attention to other
quarters.

Time passed on.   Four years had elapsed, and Henoch
ben Ezocher was still in the enjoyment of almost perfect
felicity in the companionship of his adored wife Elila.
One thing only was wanting to make their happiness
complete,—an heir; but, alas! Elila was childless.

In the mean time, old Musta had been gathered to
his fathers, and had left his entire fortune to his beloved daughter, reserving sufficient for the maintenance
of his widow, and providing that in case Elila's husband died without leaving an heir, the fortune should
be divided equally between mother and daughter.

Not long after this, the husband of Elila died also, and the young widow went back to her parental home, to mingle her tears with those of her mother in lamentation for the loved and lost.

It is a law among the Jews, observed by them all over the world, that where there are two brothers, one married and the other single, and the married brother dies, his widow, one year after her husband's death, must espouse the surviving brother, unless he release her from the obligation by a certain religious ceremony.

There was attached to the French garrison then established at El-Callah a young officer, Viscount D——. His rank was that of captain; and, although not over twenty-five years of age, he had already been decorated with the cross of the Legion of Honor of the first class. He had enjoyed the friendship of both Henoch ben Ezocher and Musta-el-Geber during their lives, and had been a frequent visitor at the home of each; and the remittances which he regularly received from his family at Lyons were paid to him through the house of Ezocher and Brother. Elila, who, like her mother, had never been subjected to the jealous surveillance so common among the Eastern nations, and had received a thorough French education, had often during the life of her husband met and conversed with the handsome French officer, who invariably treated her with the respect due to a lady and the wife of an esteemed friend.

After the death of her husband, the young viscount frequently visited Elila at her mother's residence, and, becoming convinced in the course of time that he was not without favor in her eyes, he made a formal proposal for her hand in marriage. The mother encouraged the suit by all the means in her power; and the young widow herself could not but feel flattered by the preference of the gallant and handsome Frenchman.

There was one difficulty in the way, however: the elder and unmarried brother of her deceased husband had not released the widow according to the rites of his creed; nor indeed was he willing to do so, since thereby he would lose not only the beautiful widow, but also the fortune she inherited from both her father and her husband. It is not likely that the first loss would have lain very heavily on the heart of a man who had thus far resisted the blandishments of the gentle sex, and who was totally absorbed in business; but to miss the fortune was another affair: he therefore made declaration, before the rabbi, who also acted as judge of the Jewish court, of his readiness to wed the relict of his deceased brother.

Elila had at this time just reached the age of twenty, while her brother-in-law was on the shady side of forty-five. She was independent, young, and beautiful, and, not having any particular inclination for the Jewish ceremonies and religion, she promptly refused the hand which was about to be thrust upon her, especially as she knew full well that the principal object in view was to get possession of her fortune. And there was a still stronger motive for refusal behind this: she loved the young French officer.

Thus the affair remained for some time, the brother-in-law insisting upon his claim, and Elila refusing, until at last Dame Rumor discovered that the young widow was paying frequent visits to a convent of nuns not far from her residence. Some said she was about to become a Christian, take the veil, and withdraw from the world; others were of opinion that she was preparing to be received into the Christian faith with the sole object of becoming Viscountess D——, the wife of the French captain.

These surmises reaching the ear of the elder Ezocher, he instantly demanded the calling of a Sanhedrim, composed of three rabbis of different cities, and laid before them his complaint. After considerable deliberation on the matter, Elila was summoned to come before them and make answer to the charge against her; but on the day appointed there appeared in her stead a Monsieur Lagrange, a resident French advocate, who had been employed by her, following the advice of her lover the viscount, to plead her cause. The Sanhedrim, however, refused to allow him to appear for her, and insisted that she should come in person or else suffer the penalty of imprisonment which the law empowers these courts to enforce in cases of disobedience to their commands. There being no alternative, Elila was compelled to be present.

The hall in which the rabbis held their court was crowded to repletion with a motley assemblage of spectators,—Frenchmen, Jews, Arabs, and Moors. All who could hope to gain admittance thronged to the trial of the young, beautiful, rich widow. The interest was all the greater because no case of a similar nature had ever come up before; and there was a deep anxiety to know the result.

Elila was accompanied by her lawyer, Monsieur Lagrange, by her mother, and by the administrator of her property, Asher-el-Zadi, a man who during the lifetime of her father had been one of his most intimate friends.

When she appeared in court, all present, including
the judges, gazed at her in amazement. They had expected to see the widow of their departed friend clad
in the habiliments directed by the Jewish law in cases
like hers: instead, they saw before them a woman who,
from all appearances, was one of the first French ladies
of the province.

What served still further to increase their astonishment was that Elila came before them wearing her own
hair, which, tastefully arranged, enhanced the wondrous
beauty of her countenance.

It is the custom among the Jews of Algeria and
other parts of the East to cut off the hair of a bride
on her wedding-day, just before the performance of the
marriage rite; and ever after it is forbidden to her
to be seen in public wearing her own hair: hence
the Jewish women in those countries always have a
black ribbon on their brow, which they wear under
their head-covering. Although the custom seems cruel,
and one which would be likely to disfigure them very
much, the inborn vanity of the sex has devised expe-
dients to atone for the loss of so important an ornament; and a young married woman is soon thoroughly
versed in the art of so disposing her head-dress, inter-
woven with pearls and diamonds, that the deprivation
of the hair is hardly noticeable. I have met with many
of the fair daughters of Israel, in Africa, Asia, Russia,
and Poland, where also this custom prevails; and I can
truthfully say that many of them are beautiful and
charming to excess, in spite of what a Western woman
would consider so fearful a disadvantage as the loss of
what the apostle calls the glory of the sex.

As I have said, Elila appeared in court wearing her

own hair, and this circumstance surprised the Jews present more than did her dress, and seemed to confirm the rumors which had been current respecting her visits to the convent and her intention to embrace Christianity.

Silence having been proclaimed in the court, Ezocher came forward to prefer his complaint. At that moment, the sympathies of every one present, Christian, Jew, or Arab, were entirely with the young widow; for, although the plaintiff was very little over forty-five years old, he looked as if he might be sixty. His form was bent like that of a decrepit old man, from his life-long application to the desk; his features were haggard, and avarice was depicted in every lineament. None could help pitying the tender lamb who seemed doomed to the clutches of the vulture; and the knowledge on the part of all that it was the desire to possess the inheritance rather than the widow that prompted Ezocher, served to increase the feeling against him.

As soon as the Jewish merchant had concluded his statement, the presiding rabbi requested Elila to declare her reasons for rebelling against the law of Moses in refusing to wed the brother of her deceased husband. The young widow, in a clear, silvery voice, answered that there was no obligation upon her to obey the Mosaic code, since it applied only to those who were born in the Jewish faith and educated in accordance with its precepts, while her creed had never been that of the Israelites.

A subdued exclamation of joy from one part of the audience, and of surprise from the other, resounded throughout the hall. The court called for a further explanation; but thereupon Elila's lawyer, Monsieur Lagrange, stepped forward and read an order issued by

the supreme French tribunal of Oran, which directed
that the hearing be transferred to that place. This
was accordingly done; and, as I happened to be in
Oran at the time the trial came on, I was enabled to
hear the whole of this extraordinary case.

The plaintiff being a Jew, the suit had to be opened
before a rabbi; and, as the father of the defendant had
been an Arab, the supreme tribunal of Oran had directed
that the case be tried by a rabbi and a cadi, two native
judges, a French judge being present to guarantee an
impartial decision.

The hall in which the court sat was a very fine one,
and capable of holding a large audience. On a slightly
raised platform sat the rabbi, clad in a black silk robe,
—a venerable man, with a flowing white beard that
covered the entire breadth of his chest. He occupied
the centre seat. On his right sat the cadi, an Arab of
middle age; while on his left was a judge of the
French court, dressed in the habiliments worn by the
magistrates in the courts of assizes in France.

In front of the platform was a table, at which were
seated three writers, or *chosifs*, one for each of the
judges. Their business was to record the proceedings
in the case,—the writers of the rabbi and cadi using the
Arabic language, the other using the French.

The court-room was filled with an interested crowd
of natives and Europeans; while the garrison was
fully represented, judging from the uniforms inter-
spersed throughout the assemblage. Whether it was
on account of the extraordinary nature of the case,
which had become the universal topic of conversation
in the city, or because a young and beautiful woman was
one of the principal parties, I cannot say; but certain

it is that the hall was filled long before the hour for the beginning of the trial. As for myself, I had been so fortunate as to secure a position midway between the judges' bench and the place occupied by the fair defendant.

Precisely at ten o'clock in the morning the court was opened, and the auditor introduced the case by giving a short history of the events which had led to the trial, and stating the reasons which had moved the supreme tribunal to direct the hearing to be held before a mixed court at Oran.

This done, the plaintiff was called. He related the story with which my readers are already familiar, and closed by asserting that the defendant had become the wife of his brother in accordance with the rites of the Jews, that the ceremony had been performed in synagogue, and that during the life of her husband she had conformed to all the requirements of the Jewish faith. He claimed that she was therefore bound to submit to the laws governing the conduct of the widow of a Jew, but left it with the judge of his own creed to absolve Elila from the obligation if he considered it just to do so.

Upon the conclusion of his plea, Elila was directed to make her statement. Now, however, the self-reliance which had characterized her before the court at El-Callah had vanished. Her countenance was pale, her eyes showed traces of weeping, and her whole bearing indicated a great degree of nervous excitement. At her side stood another woman, whose features were hidden by a thick veil, but whose attitude and demeanor were strongly suggestive of high rank. In a faltering voice Elila answered the preliminary questions put by the rabbi; but when he asked her to come forward and take the customary oath and remove her shoe from her foot (an essential requisite to the taking of an oath among the Jews), she became herself once more, and, in mellifluous tones, which were audible in every part of the court-room, she answered that she could not comply with the request. Then, taking from under her garment a crucifix which she had concealed there, she drew herself up with queenly dignity, and, pointing to the Christian emblem, said, "This is the only symbol upon which I can allow an oath to be administered to me."

A low murmur ran through the hall; while the rabbi, burning with indignation, rose from his seat, and, in an angry voice, declared that he had been called thither to adjudge between persons of his own creed, and could not listen to one who professed to be a Christian. For the Christians, he said, there were special tribunals; and he threatened to vacate his seat in favor of some one better entitled to sit in judgment upon the case.

At that moment the plaintiff cried out, at the top of his voice, "Believe her not! She is an impostor!— a Jewess who has but this instant become a renegade!" On hearing these words, the rabbi resumed his seat, and, with a stern look, requested Elila to state since˘ when she had become a Christian, for that on her answer depended her right to the property of her husband, and the validity of his brother's claim.

The young widow had all this time stood composed and dignified. Waiting until silence was perfectly restored, she replied, with the mien and voice of a queen, "In declaring that only upon this emblem which you

now behold could I consent to take an oath, I had no
intention of braving the judges before whom I have
been summoned to appear. That emblem stood before
me when I drew my first breath, and I was made by
baptism what is called a Christian. In childhood, I
was taught to pray before this image; and when I
arrived at years of maturity, and afflic√ion had laid its
hand upon me, I bowed before the crucifix as I sought
consolation from above. I am a Christian; and the
reason that I have been summoned before a Jewish
judge is that he who preferred the illegal complaint,
impelled by motives of avarice, has chosen to feign
ignorance of my religious views."

Once more the plaintiff, interrupting her, cried out,
"Believe her not! She is a renegade! She was married to my deceased brother in the synagogue."

"True," said Elila: "I was married in the synagogue; but before that I was married according to the
French civil code, which confers on me the right I now
claim, of refusing to be bound by the dictates of the
Jewish law." As she spoke, she unfolded a paper and
handed it to the French judge, who, after reading it,
pronounced it a marriage certificate in due form of law.
Elila was then asked to proceed, whereupon she continued:—"I am brought here to answer before a mixed
court, composed of three judges of different creeds, because my father was an Arab, my husband a Jew, and
I am a Christian."

"It is false!" once more interrupted the plaintiff.
"She was born of a Jewish mother, was educated in
the law of Moses, and was married, in conformity to
its rites, to an Israelite."

Elila now stepped aside, and her companion took

her place. It was the lady whom we have already mentioned as standing close by the young widow, and whose countenance was hidden by a thick veil. As she took the stand, she raised her veil, disclosing the features of a woman about thirty-five years old, still in the heyday of life, extremely beautiful, and bearing a marked resemblance in form and face to Elila. It was, in fact, Marhara, the mother of the defendant. The interest immediately centred upon her; for now, it was thought, would be cleared up the mystery of twenty years' standing, and the doubt that had so long enveloped the past of Madame Musta was about to be dispelled. All eyes were riveted upon her, and perfect silence reigned, that not a word of her testimony might be lost.

"My name," she began, "is Maria; my age is thirty-four; and my native country is France."

These words, pronounced in a firm and distinct tone, produced a marked effect on the audience. They had looked for an explanation of what had hitherto been a mystery, but they had not expected to hear a declaration like that just made; and, while the Christians manifested their approbation by a low murmur of applause, the Jews and Arabs stood aghast.

"When I was two years old," continued Marhara, "my parents emigrated to Morocco, where, after a residence of five years, my father died. My mother, left destitute of worldly goods, eked out a painful livelihood for herself and her child by embroidery. By the time I had reached the age of nine years, my mother's health broke down from the effects of her constant labor, and her eyesight failed, for she had been compelled to rob from her hours of sleep to earn enough

for the absolute needs of the day. Our only depend-
ence now was upon the assistance received from the
charitable; but I never obtained enough at any one
time to enable me to remain at the bedside of my sick
mother for two days in succession. Each day brought
with it the humiliating necessity of seeking from door
to door the means of warding off death by starvation.

"For three years I supported myself and my help-
less mother in this wretched way. But the burden
was to become, if possible, still heavier; for she grew
so much worse that I was forced to remain constantly
at her side throughout the day, and it was only during
the moments when sleep gave her a short respite from
her sufferings that I could steal away to solicit the
charity of passers-by. My troubles were made all the
greater by my inability to procure the remedies needful
to relieve her sufferings. Our situation became worse
daily; and the agony I experienced was indescribable.
I applied to my own countrymen; but they turned a
deaf ear to my entreaties. I made an appeal to Christians of other nations; but they told me to seek assistance from those of my own nation. I knocked at the
doors of the Arab and the Jew, and they refused to aid
me because I was a Christian. At last an old Moor,
touched by the woeful face of the child who applied
for alms night after night, directed that a portion be
given to me every evening from his own table. I went
to the French consul, and told him my mother was
dying: his reply was that he would give me a permit
for her burial as soon as I brought the requisite certificate of her decease. Such was my situation, at an age
when others are revelling in the happy visions of
childhood.

"One night, upon my return from the house of a physician whom I had entreated to visit my mother, but who had refused on account of the distance of our miserable shelter, my mother called me to her bedside. Her weakness had greatly increased since I had gone out. At first I imagined she was merely faint with hunger; but I was soon to learn that death had laid his relentless hand upon her. Her voice was barely audible, and great drops of ice-cold perspiration covered her brow. She took my hand in hers, and held it for some time without speaking. 'My poor child,' at last she said, 'I shall soon cease to be a burden upon you. After this night you will have but yourself to support; for I feel that I am about to die. You will be left alone; but your father and I will unite our prayers to the Almighty to have you in his keeping.'

"I bathed the beloved face in my tears; my heart was rent with agony; and, in a transport of grief and despair, I exclaimed, 'Oh, dearest mother, do not leave me alone; take me with you.'

"'It cannot be,' she replied. 'You must live; for you have a sacred duty to fulfil. When my spirit has taken its flight, do you go to the charitably disposed of our countrypeople and ask their aid in raising the means to commit my body to the tomb. Your tender years cannot fail to excite their sympathy, and this time you will not meet with refusals. They will do more for the dead than for the living, for it is the last good office which the poor frail body needs,—a charity which requires not to be repeated. Collect enough to bury me by the side of your father, so that my remains may not be thrown into the horrible place which is here set apart for the dead bodies of the poor. Promise

me, my darling: let my last resting-place be beside
that of my beloved husband.' She ceased to speak:
her strife with the fell tyrant was over. My mother
was dead, and I, an orphan of tender years, was left to
battle with a cold, unsympathizing world.

"The light of the lamp, which had been steadily
growing dimmer for lack of oil, was extinguished at
this instant; and in the darkness, on bended knees, I
sought consolation in my overwhelming sorrow from
Him to whom I had since earliest childhood been
taught to look as the Father of the fatherless. I remained the whole night at the bedside where lay the
mortal remains of my poor mother, vaguely hoping
that the dawn of day would prove that all had been
but a terrible dream. Alas! the stern reality soon
stared me in the face and extinguished the last glim-
mering spark of hope.

"Mindful of my deceased parent's last request, I
hastened to the consul to obtain the permit for her
burial. Once more I was doomed to be disappointed:
the certificate of a physician, and the testimony of some
competent person that my mother was a native of
France, were indispensable prerequisites. As if the
anguish I suffered, and the tears I shed, were not sufficient proof!—as if death did not carry with it its own
certificate, without requiring that of the living! In
vain, however, did I plead and protest. I was informed by the officials that misery will sometimes
feign death in order to obtain the means of prolonging
an existence that would seem to many an intolerable
burden. I left the consulate with a despairing heart.
It was impossible for me to find a physician who would
give the certificate of death; and I passed another day

and night with the remains of the dear one whom I
had lost forever. I had not tasted food for twenty-four
hours; and, faint with exhaustion and sorrow, I stretched
myself by the side of the corpse and gave myself up to
melancholy reflections. I could not weep: the fountain of tears seemed to have dried up; and my mind,
for a short time, wandered.

"At last, however, a happy thought inspired me.
Shaking off my lethargy, I went to the house of the
old Moor whose bounty had so often been the means
of keeping the breath in our bodies. To him I related
my story, not omitting to state how I had failed to
receive any assistance from the Christians. This
benevolent man procured for me the requisite papers,
and I at once proceeded to the consulate to obtain the
burial-permit. This time there was no difficulty; and
as soon as the permit was placed in my hands, I sped
back to our wretched home, as joyfully as though I
had become heir to a vast fortune, and, entering the
dismal room, exclaimed, 'Here, dear mother, is all that
is needed!' Then, in an instant coming back to my
reason, I fully realized the nature of my prize,—a document allowing the dead body of my only earthly friend
to be laid in the silent grave!

"The cemetery where my father lay buried was not
far from our abode. It is a spot set apart for the reception of the bodies of deceased foreigners whose
friends can pay a certain tax for the privilege of using
six feet of ground in the land of the infidel. Present-
ing the paper which I had obtained with so much
trouble, I asked that the grave be dug near that of my
father; but my request was denied, for the permit
assigned my mother to that part of the ground into

which are thrown the bodies of all who are destitute of means, friends, or name."

Here the speaker paused. The sorrowful recollections of the past seemed to overpower her; her voice was choked with sobs, and her face bathed in tears. After giving way to her grief for a few moments, she composed herself by a powerful effort, and continued her narrative :—

"My despair had now reached its climax; and I returned, bewildered and hopeless, to the place I had called my home, again to commune with the dead. On my arrival there, a new and unlooked-for sorrow was added to those which already bowed me to the earth. The police had been summoned by some Christian neighbor, who feared the dead more than he did the living, to remove the nuisance, as my poor mother's corpse was denominated by them. To save from desecration the remains of her who had given me life, I had recourse to a lie. I told the officials that all the necessary arrangements had been made, and that on the following morning the hearse would arrive to convey the body to the foreign burial-ground. Fortunately, they credited my story, and I was once more left alone with my precious dead. When all had departed, I became fully impressed with my responsibility, and, kneeling at my mother's side, I made a solemn vow to fulfil her dying request, and lay her by the side of the husband whom she had loved so well, should it even be necessary to dig the grave at midnight with my own hands.

"At once I set out, with all the excitements of the past hour strong upon me, towards a street in which, as I had learned from others of my own sex, lived a

man who traded in human flesh, and who paid liberally
for young girls of foreign birth.   Fortune at last
seemed disposed to smile upon me; for when I arrived
at his house the commodity was scarce, and at that very
instant a rich Arab, who was on his return to Algeria,
his native land, was in quest of some fair damsel to accompany him.   I happened to be the piece of merchandise that best suited his fancy; and all I demanded was
enough to enable me to bury, with due respect, the remains of my mother.   The Arab at once paid the price,
and thus my mother's last request was fulfilled, and she
now lies by the side of her husband in the foreigners'
cemetery at Morocco.

"The object for which I had struggled so long having
been achieved, my overtaxed system gave way, and sick-
ness and delirium seized me.   Musta-el-Geber,—for he it
was,—pleased with the filial spirit I had displayed, be-
stowed the tenderest care upon me; and as soon as my
health was restored I accompanied him to Algiers, and
thence to his home at El-Callah, where I became his
wife,—if not by the forms of what is called law, at
least by the ties of love and gratitude.   The sole issue
of this connection is my daughter Elila, this day summoned before you."

The audience, who had listened to this interesting
narrative with profound attention, many of them having even been moved to tears at the recital of her woes,
now burst into enthusiastic applause, and the friends
of Marhara pressed towards the witness-stand to con-
gratulate her on her effective statement of the incidents
of her early life.

After a short consultation between the judges, the
French judge declared the verdict of the court to be in

Elila's favor, absolving her from all obligation to the requisitions of the Hebrew faith.

Once more the room resounded with the applause of the delighted spectators; and Elila and her mother were conducted from the precincts of the court by their friends and led in triumph through the streets of Oran.

A fortnight afterwards, the judge who announced the decision of the court in this suit had another duty to perform,—which was, to register the names of Viscount D—— and Elila Musta as those of man and wife.

The above being an extraordinary case, a mixed court had been formed, adhering in the main to European customs; but in ordinary suits in Algerine courts the native judges preside, who sit cross-legged, seldom looking at the contestants, but continually turning over the leaves of the Koran, which lies open before them, as though they were searching for something that might throw light on the matter in hand. This, however, I was afterwards informed, was a piece of mere formality; for very many of the native judges can neither read nor write. If the complainant be a male, he makes his statement in a sitting posture, similar to that of the judges; while females are heard through a latticed window somewhat resembling a confessional.

In the description of the trial I made mention, as the reader will remember, of a heavy veil covering the features of Marhara. A few words on this subject may not be amiss here. The veil of an Arab woman is often worn with a great deal of coquetry, and according to the manner in which she wears it is the stranger to judge whether she is beautiful or otherwise. If she is of comely countenance, the veil is of very fine texture, and arranged tastefully in such a manner as to permit the features to be seen. If she meets a member of the sterner sex in whom she feels sufficiently interested to desire to exhibit her face, she lifts her *foutah*,—the veil that forms the upper part of her head-dress,—as if with the purpose of arranging it, so that the person for whose benefit this coquettish ruse is practised may have a full view of her features. With the single exception of this custom, prompted by a harmless vanity, there is nothing in the conduct of the Arab women which the severest moralist could find occasion to rebuke.

They use the dye of the gall-nut to give definiteness to the line that joins the eyebrows, and color their eyelids with antimony. Their finger-nails they stain with henna, which imparts to them a by no means disagreeable shade of brown.

At Oran I formed the acquaintance of an Arab who invited me, with some friends, to visit him at his home. At the appointed hour I presented myself, and was admitted by a Moorish woman past the summer of life. She was unveiled; but I should have preferred seeing her abide by the custom of the country, and leave the abandonment of the face-covering to the younger women.

This absurd custom of wearing a veil prevails among the Moorish women of northern Africa; but, as in Europe and America, it is generally only the young and beautiful who jealously cover their faces from the admiration of the world. When the traveller in Algeria sees at a distance a woman in the street without a veil, he may feel tolerably certain that she is either long past the prime of life, or that, if young, she is entirely devoid of the charms of beauty.

In the visit to the house of the Arab of whom I have just spoken, a capital opportunity was afforded me of seeing the Moorish women unveiled. Upon our arrival at the place, we had to mount to the second story, and from thence clamber to the top of the house by means of a wooden ladder. The master being absent, we were requested to await his coming, and were served with couches, coffee, and pipes, in the garden on the roof, to make the time pass agreeably.

The flat roofs of the neighboring houses were crowded with women, all unveiled, their beautiful long hair arranged on the top of their heads and tied with ribbons of all colors. Their merry laughter reminded me of the scenes I had often witnessed at large boarding-schools when the pupils were enjoying a recess in the open air. As nearly all the houses in Oran are white-washed, the variegated colors of the women's trousers seemed all the brighter for the background, and added greatly to the effect of the whole picture. The fair Moors were by no means displeased at our admiring glances: they seemed glad to be seen unveiled, as what woman does not who possesses any charms?

The Arabs of Algiers differ widely in their customs from those of the south. The peculiarities of the former, in consequence of their constant intercourse with foreigners, have become greatly modified; the latter still adhere strictly to the habits of their ancestors.

There is a class of Arabs that might be styled a mongrel race, having become so from intermixture with tribes of other nations. Although there is a great difference between them and the classes mentioned above, yet in many of them the degrees of transition may easily be traced.

11*

Several of the Kabyl tribes whom I met in the province of Constantine speak the Arabic; and among those in the neighborhood of Ghelma the physiognomy, language, and customs of the Arab predominate. The tribe of the Amrauhs, near Dellys, is half Arabic, half Berber; and the Moors of Mascara have many of the Arab traits. The Moors who are driven from their homes by the perpetual wars that devastate the country are forced to seek refuge among the Arabs of the wilderness, and soon become affiliated with the desert wanderers by community of habits or by intermarriage; and especially has this been the case since the French have taken possession of the country.

But, while the Moor or the Kabyl readily intermingles with the Arab, it is very rarely that the latter casts in his lot with any but his own people; and on this account the Arab population is the most homogeneous and vigorous of the races that inhabit Barbary, and the one which has departed the least from its original type. They are divided into several classes. Those who occupy settled abodes apply themselves to agriculture or commerce; while the nomad Arab, or Bedouin, is a stock-breeder, and very frequently a robber. The word Bedouin comes from *Bedavi*, which means, in Arabic, countrypeople. The Arabs who are settled in towns and villages are few in number, and are styled " Kadars" (villagers, or citizens). The true Bedouins are found only in the Beled-el-Jerid (Land of Dates), in the Kobla (South), and on the confines of the Great Desert. They lead a wandering life, roving from one part of the country to another in search of the best pasture for their camels and their large flocks of sheep.

The Arabs of Barbary speak a dialect of the pure Arabic, which the Egyptians understand with difficulty, and which is wholly unintelligible to the Syrians and the inhabitants of the great peninsula.

Before resuming my journey to Tlemcen, I visited a *duar*, about fifteen miles from Oran. The term *duar* is the Arabic equivalent for a circuit, or, perhaps I may more correctly say, a village. This one consisted of some three hundred tents, pitched in the form of a large circle, in the centre of which was a spacious enclosure for the cattle. These tents are made of black camel-hair, and are so constructed that they can be moved from place to place with great facility. A *duar* of from three hundred to four hundred tents can be removed in about thirty minutes. Of late years, however, a few of the tribes, such as the Beni Khalil, in the vicinity of Algiers, have abandoned the tents for miserable straw huts, which they call *gurbi*. These huts are grouped in a circle like the tents, and collectively are termed *jeenahs* if situated in the plains, and *dashkrahs* if on the mountains.

I obtained permission to enter one of these tents, which certainly did not present any great attractions on the score of cleanliness. The interior I found partitioned off into two apartments by a curtain of the same material as that which composed the tent. The moment I entered, the female inmates withdrew, as is their invariable custom when their lord receives a male visitor; notwithstanding which, they are by no means reluctant to be seen by a stranger, particularly if he be a foreigner. With one glance I took an inventory of the furniture, which consisted of a few palm-leaf mats, several sheepskins serving as quilts, for use when the nights are uncomfortably cool, and a few rude earthen jugs for holding water, milk, &c.

From the sides of the tent were suspended a few household utensils, some firearms, and the gear for the horses; and in one corner was an apparatus for grinding corn, which looked old-fashioned enough to have been invented just after the Flood. Another corner was set apart as a wardrobe, which, however, displayed no great variety of garments, since the code of fashion has no dominion among the sons of the desert. Their entire outfit consists of a white robe, called *Kaikh*, or dress, covering the body from neck to ankles. The ordinary Arab wears his closely fitting to the skin; those who are blessed with a better share of worldly goods have a sort of under-garment, over which is worn a broad kaikh, fastened to the bald head by a reddish-brown cord of camel's hair and serving as a turban as well as a covering for the body.

This shirt—if we may so call it—is made of fine wool. Next comes a wide *burnous*, of coarser material than the kaikh, sometimes white, sometimes black. The *capuz*, or cowl, serves the purpose of an umbrella. The burnous screens their bare legs; while on the feet they wear a piece of oxhide, tied with strings, except among the better class, who wear high boots of yellow or reddish leather.

After I had been offered the pipe and a cup of coffee, and had informed the master of the tent that I was not a Frenchman,—a very agreeable piece of news to him, apparently,—I ventured to ask permission to see his family,—meaning thereby, of course, the ladies; for I cared not a whit about looking at his sons, babies, or grandchildren, if he had any. He hesitated for a few moments, but at last said, "Allah Kerim" ("God is merciful"), and, without informing me whether my request was to be acceded to or not, abruptly left me and went into the other apartment. After a short interval, he again made his appearance, accompanied by eight women, all dressed in wide woollen shirts with short sleeves.

The sight of these wives and daughters of a nomad Arab was an exceedingly interesting one to me from its novelty. Their hair had a disordered look; that is to say, it did not lie smooth, as though it had been carefully brushed, but presented the appearance that we may behold in the natural head-covering of some of our fashionable sisters in the Western world,—that of studied negligence. It was braided into two long tresses; and the elder women had decorated theirs with fragments of bright-colored handkerchiefs. The legs, breasts, and faces of those over thirty years of age were tattooed; those under that age were free from the hideous disfiguration. The latter appeared to me quite handsome, with their regular features and large black eyes; but no female face is beautiful to a native until it has been tattooed. All of them, old and young, had their finger-nails dyed a reddish-brown with henna. On their well-proportioned arms and ankles they wore thick clasps of brass, which they evidently took great care to keep bright and polished. Their ears were adorned with enormous rings, this style of ornamentation being one of the special luxuries of the women in that part of the country.

A very common but erroneous impression is that no Arab woman is allowed to appear unveiled in the presence of a stranger. It is true, the Koran enjoins the use of the veil in all such cases; but the injunction is observed by none but the wives of the marabouts, the only class that rigidly adheres to the precepts of Mohammed.

Upon the entrance of the women, my European instincts would have caused me at once to rise from the mat upon which I was seated, but that the master of the tent made a motion requesting me to retain my position. The eight women, then, were all standing before me, without a word passing on either side. I looked for a formal introduction to Mrs. and the Misses Arab; but none came; and all I could do was to review the party in silence from head to foot, and then bow my head as a sign of thanks. They thereupon retired to the inner apartment, but could not refrain from peeping slyly every now and then at the stranger who had been so anxious to make their acquaintance.

I mentioned to my host that I had left Oran rather hurriedly, and without having looked for some one who could furnish me with a letter of introduction, but that I was very desirous to become acquainted with the Arab customs and tent-life, and should be glad to be allowed to remain among them for a short time.

It is asserted by some that the Arabs are hospitable to none but those of their own creed, and that foreigners who do not come well recommended are frequently obliged to leave their encampments without having been afforded the opportunity of gratifying their curiosity. My experience, however, teaches the reverse of this; for I had no sooner expressed my wish than my host tendered me the hospitality of his tent for any length of time I chose to stay among his people; and I very gladly accepted his kind offer.

Knowing that the Arab, like his fellow-men in other quarters of the world than Algeria, can be bought by presents, or that at least his friendship will grow none the cooler if you manifest by a few gifts your appreciation of his services, I began to cast about me for the means of propitiating my host. I had left my trunk at Oran, and had nothing with me but cigars and a little money: I therefore presented him, at the same time warmly thanking him for his hospitality, with as many five-franc pieces as there were women in the family, begging him to give one to each of them. I soon found I had acted a prudent part; for the Arab's face beamed with pleasure, and his offers of service and hospitality were redoubled.

Towards evening I took a stroll through the *jubar*, or tents. Children were sporting in front of the greater number; while here and there a woman was to be seen, coming from the enclosure where the cattle are kept, carrying milk to the tent of her husband, or performing some other duty appertaining to the weaker sex. The women here do all the household work; the men attend to the field and all other hard labor. In their domestic life there is no affection manifested between man and wife. I would not, however, have the reader infer from this that the women are ill treated by the men; for such is by no means the case, and cruelty on the part of an Arab towards his wife would be followed by summary punishment and a separation.

As I was sauntering along, I was joined by my new-made Arab friend, who invited me to pay a visit to the sheik, who was at the same time the judge of the duar. The sheik of each of these tent-villages is not only the judge in all disputes that require arbitration, but is also the military commander of the population. His rank and office are hereditary.

Ordinarily, twenty or thirty of these duars form a tribe; but the tribe which I visited—situated in one of the most fertile regions of Algeria and known by the name of Beni Hamdan (sons of Hamdan)—consisted of one hundred and eighteen duars. The chief of the tribe, called Kaid, resided at another and much larger duar.

As we threaded our way between the tents, I could very easily distinguish the residence of the sheik. It was built of stone, and stood in the centre of a small lawn surrounded by trees and a hedge of cactus. Arrived at his house, we were told that he was absent, in attendance upon a meeting; for at all meetings the sheik presides, and interferes when difficulties arise. This tribe was so large that on a certain occasion, not very far back, the *kaid*, or chief, led more than three thousand horsemen to battle.

Having been thus disappointed in seeing the sheik, we resolved to visit the second in authority, namely, the *marabout*, or high-priest. But every priest is not a marabout, nor is every marabout a priest.

The marabouts are a class of men who profess to lead a holy life, minutely observe the precepts of the Koran, and deny themselves the enjoyment of worldly pleasures. They remind me of the monks of olden time, and are held in extreme veneration by their co-religionists on account of the blamelessness of their lives, their charitable actions, and their supposed wisdom. They are generally able to read and write, and know how to explain the Koran. The majority of them live in seclusion, abstain from smoking, and set an example of the suppression of all the baser passions. The learned marabouts are the professors who instruct youth, preside over seminaries, and deliver lectures, which are often attended by crowds of the followers of the Prophet. The abodes of such of them as are hermits are considered sacred and inviolable; and the criminal, no matter what his offence, who manages to escape from justice and place himself under the protection of an anchorite marabout is safe: not the most powerful of the chiefs would dare to molest him.

Some of these marabouts are really good men; but the greater part are mere impostors, professing to have the power to see into futurity; and, generally, the more absurd and unfounded their claims to consideration and the more unreasonable their actions, the more money do they draw from the faithful.

We found the marabout of the duar in front of his tent, engaged in conversation; and when I was presented to him he stretched out his hand and gave me a kind welcome. After explaining to the holy man the object of my visit, my host took his leave, promising to meet me at his tent.

After the customary *Wash halek wash hinta* (" How do you do ?") of the other Arabs present, we all seated ourselves, and conversation immediately turned upon myself,—whence I came, what was my occupation, &c. I told them all I could truthfully say without disparaging myself; and as soon as they heard I was a *taleb* (doctor) they rose and saluted me reverentially.

Among the Mozabites—that is, the Arabs who live in the oases—the medical profession is held in high repute: the taleb is with them at once Kaid, Sheik, and Marabout: he is the chief of the tribe, whose every word

is law, and who is universally obeyed. Among the
Arabs of Algeria the talebs do not occupy so high a
position as among the Mozabites; but they are looked
upon with great respect, and even a European taleb is
with them a man of consideration, though not in the
same degree as a native.

The marabout of the duar I was visiting was a vene-
rable-looking Arab, who, although there was no distinction in dress between him and the others, could at
once be recognized as of superior rank, from the respect
shown to him by all.

Sidi Mehemet,—so he was named,—I ascertained
during our talk, was a historical character; and I will
here relate one of the incidents of his life. Three
years before my visit to Algiers, a Kabyl tribe that had
temporarily taken up its abode in the Atlas Mountains
was shamefully maltreated by certain subordinate French
officers; and as the natives found it impossible to obtain redress from the superior in command, they resolved to take the punishment into their own hands.
One day, therefore, when the French least expected it,
the Kabyls poured down upon them from their moun-
tain-home with the fury of an avalanche, and made
fearful havoc among the detachments stationed at various points along the base of the Atlas range.

Sidi Mehemet lived among the tribe that had re-
volted, and, before the occurrence of which I am speaking, had done many a friendly service to French prisoners. Many of the *Rummis* (Christians) who refused
to become Islamites were ill treated on that account by
the natives, until Sidi Mehemet, taking pity on the
miserable condition of the captives, extended to them
his protection.

One of these prisoners was an Alsatian soldier, who had been condemned to be put to death and was saved only by the intervention of Sidi Mehemet. This act of kindness was never forgotten by the French soldier, who at the time of the outbreak of which I have spoken had risen to the rank of captain.

General Pelissier, then stationed at Algiers, went in pursuit of the insurgent Kabyls, who, finding themselves driven into the innermost recesses of the mountain, retreated with their wives and children to a cave which was large enough to hold double their number.

They here thought themselves secure. The next day, however, the French had ferreted them out, and were drawn up in front of the entrance.

The determination of the Kabyls to defend themselves to the last extremity never wavered, especially as they knew that the foe could not remain long in the wild mountain-passes. Many a brave Kabyl fell in the contest; but his wife immediately took up his musket and fought in his stead.

They had ammunition and food enough to last for three days; and at the expiration of that time, they hoped, the assailants would be obliged to retire.

The French, seeing at last that they could not force an entrance, and unwilling to remain long in a region where reinforcements for the enemy might arrive at any moment, determined on a measure which they thought would soon bring the Kabyls to terms.

An immense heap of brushwood was collected and piled up before the mouth of the cave. The Kabyls were then summoned to surrender, or the brushwood would be set on fire and every soul of them must perish. The Kabyls, however, sternly refused to listen to any terms; and, although they well knew the terrible fate in store for them, they thought it better to die at once like heroes than to suffer the humiliation inseparable from capture by the French.

At this critical moment Sidi Mehemet, the marabout, came forth. His object was to intercede with the Europeans; although the men in the cave had given no intimation of a desire to surrender. His pleadings were of no avail; and upon being informed of the determination of Pelissier to set fire to the accumulated combustibles in front of the cave, he asked permission to go back, that he might share the fate of his countrymen, rather than abandon them when they most needed to hear the words of the Koran. His request was granted; but just as he was stepping into the cave a strong hand was laid on his shoulder, with the announcement that he was a prisoner; and he was at once taken to a distance from the horrible scene which so sullied the pages of the history of the French conquest of Algiers.

The officer who claimed the marabout as prisoner was the Alsatian soldier who had been rescued from death by Sidi Mehemet. He had recognized in the marabout his benefactor, and, desirous of making some return for the Arab's former good offices, had taken him prisoner with the purpose of saving him from a horrible death.

A few moments after, the torch was applied to the combustibles, and the smoke that entered the cave warned its defenders of the fate that was in store for them.

Until now there had been some hope of their surrender; but the chant of certain favorite verses of the Koran, heard from within, apprized the French that the Kabyls were resolved to die. Here was an opportunity for Pelissier to display the magnanimity of the chivalrous soldier, and thus to have decorated his breast with a star brighter and more enduring than that of the "Légion d'Honneur." But no: the transitory fame of a French general was of more value, in his eyes, than the lives of a few Arabs. The fire was kept up, and the whole tribe, consisting of nearly five hundred persons, men, women, and children, perished by suffocation. They died the death of heroes, rather than lose their independence by surrendering to their enemies; while Pelissier took upon his soul the guilt of the wholesale butchery of a tribe, rather than return to his encampment without being able to record another *glorious* victory over the insurgent Arabs.

It would occupy much more space than I can afford, were I to relate the story in the words of the marabout, who had witnessed the whole of the horrible massacre. Seeing the sympathy expressed in my features and receiving my congratulations on his own escape, he sprang from his seat, and, his large black eyes kindling with enthusiasm, grasped my hand, exclaiming, "You are not a Frenchman,—your sympathy is not affected; I read it in your face; for there I cannot discover the traits of a hypocrite."

This incident established the fullest confidence between the marabout and myself; and, knowing the veneration with which he was regarded by his people, I had no longer any doubts as to my safety while among them.

The men with whom he had been talking before I was introduced to him, following the example of the marabout, welcomed me to their settlement; and, having become accustomed, in my frequent wanderings, to adapt myself to almost any mode of life, I was soon perfectly "at home" among these semi-barbarous nomads. Each of the party offered me his tent to make it my home during my sojourn,—the marabout as freely as the others. I declined their invitations, with many thanks, stating that I had already accepted the hospitality of the Arab who had introduced me to them. No greater affront can be offered to one of these people than to leave his residence, once you have become his guest, and take up your abode with some one else. They at once admitted the force of my excuse, and seemed very much pleased at my respect for their customs. The evening being now pretty well advanced, I bade them good-evening, promising to make a visit to each of them the next day.

When I returned to the tent of my host, I found him waiting for me outside, engaged in conversation with some neighbors, of whom he took leave the instant he saw me, and entered the tent along with me, remarking that my repast had been in waiting for some time.

Among these people a guest is served first, as a mark of honor; then the father, sons, and other male members of the family participate, all eating from the same dish; last of all come the mother and daughters, with the other female relations. While the men are partaking, the women look on silently at a distance.

The principal dish—in fact, the only one—consisted of the *Kuskusu*, somewhat resembling a pudding, and made of small globules of a paste prepared from wheat by an operation peculiar to the Arabs. Raisins and currants were mixed with the one served on this occasion, and over the whole was poured a sort of broth made of sweetened milk. A hole in the centre was filled with butter; and on the top of the dish was a roast fowl, divided into suitable portions. This last adjunct is met with only on extraordinary occasions, except at the table of the rich Arabs, where the *Kuskusu* never appears without it.

This dish disposed of, we were served with fruits, consisting of dates and fresh-picked prickly-pears,—the latter of which are delicious in all parts of Algeria. Coffee was brought on, as among us, at the close of the meal.

After our repast, the time until the hour of repose was spent agreeably in conversation with my host. Having, in the course of my travels, become accustomed to all sorts of beds, I found it no hardship to compose myself to slumber on a few mats; and I slept as soundly as though I had been among the friends of a lifetime. Although an unbeliever,—a *Rummi*, as all Christians are styled by the Arabs,—with from eight hundred to a thousand half-savage men around me, I was without any uneasy feeling that the *yataghan* of some zealous Mohammedan might change the slumber of the Christian stranger into the sleep that knows no waking.

The male members of the family occupied the apartment with me; the females retired to the inner room, partitioned off from the rest of the tent by a curtain, as I have before explained.

When I awoke in the morning, I found that the men had all left the tent before me, and that the women alone remained, busied about their household affairs. I deliberated with myself as to the propriety of asking a question or two, not knowing whether or not it would be a breach of etiquette to address any of the women, and not wishing to infringe any of their customs, nor to do any thing that might cause my host to regret having tendered me the shelter of his roof. While in this uncertainty, a daughter of the family made her appearance, offering me a cup of hot coffee; and, as she addressed me first, my problem was solved. She was a talkative little creature, and, although not more than fifteen, was the mother of two children; for among the Arabs the girls marry at eleven or twelve, and at the age of thirty they are generally grandmothers. This state of things is quite common in Africa; but why should we wonder at it, when the same barbarous custom is practised in Europe and tolerated by the most civilized governments of the Western hemisphere?

Apropos of this subject I must beg the reader's permission to relate what I witnessed during my earlier years while on a journey through Poland; and I trust it will interest him sufficiently to atone for transporting him *sans cérémonie* from the warm plains of Africa to the bleak regions of northern Europe.

It was in the year 1846. The university at Pesth had closed its doors for two months, and I availed myself of the vacation to make a trip on the Danube to the celebrated fortress of Comorn, thence along the Waag to Neustadtl, thence to the renowned ruins of Trentschin, and from Trentschin by way of Huntsdorf across the Carpathians into Galicia, visiting the celebrated salt-mines of Wieliczka and Bochnia.

At Podzorze, a city that is separated from Cracow by the Vistula, I happened to make the acquaintance of a Polish noble who had large possessions in Galicia, or Austrian Poland, situated in the neighborhood of Lemberg. He invited me to travel in company with him; and, as at that time I was not encumbered with a super-abundance of cash, and was really glad to meet a pleasant companion with whom I could travel and be at the same time free from the necessity of drawing too heavily on my meagre purse, he did not find it needful to ask the question a second time.

Pan Wynowsky was a young man, about six years my senior, and had just returned from Warsaw, whither he had been to visit his wife, who was staying there for a short time with her parents.

He was travelling, as was the custom in that part of the country, in his own chaise, changing post-horses at each station. This, by the way, was the cheapest and most commodious method of travelling: a fixed price was paid for each mile, and there was sure to be no detention on the road either by day or by night. But, then, this mode of travel could be enjoyed by none but a certain privileged class; for post-horses were supplied only to those who had obtained, from the authorities of the place from whence they started, a certain document giving them the right to that advantage.

This kind of travel reminds me of an incident that led to the elevation of a poor but beautiful girl, the daughter of a village postmaster, to the rank of a princess of the house of Austria.

The Archduke Albert, brother of the late Emperor Ferdinand of Austria, who abdicated in favor of his nephew, the present emperor, was once travelling in Upper Austria by post, in the manner above described.

At that time railroads were not known in Upper Austria; and, as the archduke was anxious to reach Vienna as soon as possible, where his presence was required at a family council, he travelled day and night incognito, so as not to be detained by the homage of the authorities in the villages and cities through which he had to pass.

It is the custom of the postilion to blow a horn before he arrives at the next station, to give notice to the people there to have fresh horses ready to be harnessed in at once, that the journey may continue without delay.

The archduke had just arrived at an insignificant little village; the signal had been given, but there was no fresh relay. On the traveller's impatiently demanding the cause, the postmaster excused himself on the plea that, although he had the horses, there was nobody to lead them; for all his men were out with different relays with passengers who had arrived a short time before.

Much vexed by this unexpected delay, the archduke offered to pay a large reward if a postilion were procured; but all in vain, the postmaster being infirm, and there being no other man in the house at the time.

Although ignorant of the rank of the archduke, yet, feeling a desire to oblige him, the postmaster went to the next room, with the intention of sending his only daughter, a girl not more than sixteen years of age, to look for somebody in the neighborhood who might serve as postilion. The daughter had overheard the conversation between her father and the traveller, the door between the rooms being open. She proposed to her father to let her undertake the service herself. His consent obtained, she changed her garments for those of the postilion, and before many minutes had elapsed she had mounted the dicky and was ready to start.

Off drove the post-chaise; and the archduke could not but admire the beautiful boy who was driving, and who seemed lost in the high boots, the buckskin trousers, the silver-buttoned red jockey-coat, and three-cornered hat of the postilion. Entering into conversation with him, he was not a little surprised to find that it was the daughter of the postmaster who had thus aided him out of a difficulty.

Being of a somewhat adventurous and amorous disposition, he left his comfortable seat and placed himself beside the postilion. One word led to another, until he began to complain of the speed with which she drove the horses; for now he felt as if he did not care to reach his destination at all. But the horses, in spite of all slackening of their pace, soon arrived at the next station, and, taking leave there of the young girl, the archduke promised to come and see her again before long, giving her at the same time a handsome present.

A fortnight afterwards, the same stranger presented himself at the house of his *belle postillon*, and, giving a fictitious name, demanded her hand in marriage. The father, delighted at the unlooked-for good fortune which had befallen his daughter, and by which he expected to better his own condition, interposed very few obstacles; and three days afterwards the fair postilion was united to the archduke, who went under the name of Albert Baron von Bamberg. His wife was not aware of her real position until, upon her arrival at Innspruck, the capital of Tyrol, she was conducted by her husband to his archducal palace.

As it is not my object here to relate how the court of

Austria received the news of this *mésalliance*, I will return to my Polish friend in whose company I intended to make a trip to Lemberg.

After having visited in Cracow the celebrated chapel of Prince Poniatowsky, erected in memory of the ill-fated Pole who lost his life, as one of Napoleon's generals, at the battle of Leipsic and found a watery grave in the Elbe, we resolved to start for Wieliczka.

Space would fail me, even had I the ability, to give an adequate description of the celebrated salt-mines at this place. Enough to say that we spent three days in them; and as for myself, I could have stayed there for weeks, so deeply interesting did I find the sculpture and architecture cut out of the salt rock at a depth of two thousand feet below the surface.

From Wieliczka we went to Bochnia, distant about seven German miles (equal to about twenty-seven English miles). Here also we visited the mines. The stratum of salt worked here is the same as the one worked at Wieliczka; and at the time of my visit the passages of the two mines would have met if prolonged sufficiently in the direction which the miners were pursuing: the extremities, indeed, were not more than five miles apart.

From Bochnia we went to Tarnof, the largest city in Galicia except Lemberg. We left Tarnof on a Saturday afternoon, and before night a storm arose, accompanied with such heavy rain that we determined to stop at the first place we came to, and, if there was any likelihood of finding accommodations, remain there over night. Happily, we were not far from a little town called Jablouka; and we directed the coachman to stop at the first hotel he should come to.

The word hotel, however, is not known in that part

of the country: all public houses are called taverns, and are invariably kept by Jews.

It was nine o'clock at night when we entered the tavern. The house was a one-story structure, and was divided into four apartments. No. 1 was the kitchen, which served also for the domestics, poor travellers, drivers, and the servants of wealthy passengers. Next came the store-room, filled with bags of grain, which had accumulated there during the week, to be carried to market on the following Tuesday, that being the day of the general fair for all the traders of the neighborhood. No. 3 was occupied by the proprietor and his unmarried daughters; while the fourth was hall, parlor, sleeping-room, exchange, and reception-room, all in one. This is the invariable plan on which all public houses in this region are built.

At the first glance, this room, on account of the numerous screens it contains, looks like a hospital; but it is nothing of the kind. Behind these screens are the sleeping-apartments of the married daughters and sons of the proprietor. The furniture in each compartment consists of one bed, serving for the children as well as the parents; at the foot of the bed hang their wardrobe and a small looking-glass, while the pitcher and basin occupy a corner under the bed; near the looking-glass is a towel, that is replaced every Saturday.

In the centre of the room is a rough table, made of unpainted pine boards; and on both sides are benches, which, together with the table, extend the whole length of the apartment.

This is the only table in the house, and serves a great variety of purposes. If the Jew makes a bargain, here the money is counted down; at the regular,

or rather irregular, meal-hours, dishes are served here
in earthen vessels, without a table-cloth ever being
spread upon it, except on extraordinary occasions. It is
also the common writing-desk, and serves to support the
ponderous volumes of the Talmud, placed there by the
young married men, who endeavor to improve their
minds by reading them daily. Every morning at
six o'clock, the whole family, from the eldest to the
youngest who is able to read, unite around this table
for more than an hour, to read their prayers. Notwithstanding the lack of all the appliances which among
Christians are considered essential to comfort, the
proprietor of a tavern like the one I am describing is
sometimes worth from a hundred to two hundred thousand *golden*.

As we had arrived late at night, one of the beds
behind the screen was offered to us; but, being reluctant to disturb the occupants, we chose the hard
table for a sleeping-place, making it as comfortable as
possible by using the cushions of the post-chaise for
pillows. Our slumbers, however, were far from being
unbroken; for we were treated to a juvenile concert of
such a variety of voices that it was impossible to enjoy
a quiet sleep. There were not less than a dozen of
these youngsters stowed away with their respective
parents behind the screens.

On the following morning, as it was Sunday and the
weather was still unfavorable, we decided to remain
until noon. At an early hour we sallied out to inspect
the town,—the atmosphere of the crowded room being
any thing but pleasant,—ordering breakfast to be ready
for us by our return. Upon re-entering the room at
about nine o'clock, we were surprised to see the inmates

all dressed in gala costume, knowing as we did that this was not the Sabbath-day of the Israelites. The men had on beaver-skin hats, something like those worn by the Russian Cossacks; then came a cloak of black satin, which reached from the neck to the ankles, resembling the *togas* worn by Roman Catholic priests, especially those of Spain. Under this cloak were a vest and tight breeches of the same material. Some of the company had on black silk stockings, and others white; and the shoes of all were adorned with silver buckles.

According to the Mosaic religion, the Jew is not permitted to touch his face with a razor: the Polish Jew, therefore, allows his beard to grow, cutting it once a year with scissors: many, indeed, never cut it at all. Those of other parts of the globe who are averse to wearing beards and are yet unwilling to infringe the law, use once a week (generally upon the eve of their Sabbath-day) a composition of quicklime and *aurum pigmentum*, which, after being boiled so as to form a paste, is spread with a wooden knife on that part of the face where the hair grows, and allowed to remain there for five minutes. It is then washed off with cold water, and the face is left as smooth as that of a new-born babe. Treated in this manner, the beard does not grow so rapidly as when subjected to the constant use of the razor.

The dress of the females is quite a contrast to that of the men. The same law which forbids the men to shave their beards prohibits the women from preserving their luxuriant tresses, which are shorn from their heads upon the day of their marriage: thenceforward they are not permitted to allow the hair to grow, while until that time they wear it in profuse ringlets around their necks. To obviate as far as possible the want of this natural adornment, they wear rich turbans, which among the higher classes are thickly studded with pearls, diamonds, and all kinds of precious stones, and from beneath this head-gear hang clustering ringlets of fine silk. The skirts of their dresses are short, and made of the richest materials, such as silk and satin, of brilliant hues; while over a bright-colored bodice they wear a jacket similar in pattern to the Zouave. Their small and well-shaped feet are encased in neatly-fitting shoes adorned with buckles; and they let slip no opportunity to display coquettishly the contour of their gracefully-turned ankles.

If the dress of the adult members of the family was to us a curious sight, much more so was that of the younger ones, who, although the oldest of them was not more than ten years of age, were attired in the same style as their elders.

Inquiring into the cause of what seemed to us an un-usual parade, we were informed by the proprietor that one of his sons was to be married that day, and were kindly invited to be present at the ceremony, if our engagements permitted. As a marriage-celebration among these people was a thorough novelty to us, we gladly accepted the invitation, at the same time express-ing a desire to be made acquainted with the bride-groom. At a nod from our host, that happy individual stood before us,—when, to our astonishment, we beheld a mere lad, who had not yet completed his fourteenth year, and who, it seemed, was still attending one of the Jewish schools in the neighborhood. The father of the bridegroom, seeing that our curiosity was aroused, entered into a lengthy explanation, the substance of which was as follows.

Marriages, among these people, are arranged by the parents, without any consultation of the wishes of the parties who are chiefly interested. The children are looked upon simply as so many pieces of merchandise, to be disposed of at the pleasure of the owner. The marriage-contracts are usually concluded on regular market-days. For instance, a merchant takes a wagon-load of grain to market, to be sold to the highest bidder. The moment a purchaser is found, the grain is transferred to him, and buyer and seller start for the nearest tavern to count over the money. This done, they enter into general conversation, and make inquiries relating to each other's family; and if it turn out that one of them has a marriageable daughter,—that is, one who has reached the age of twelve years,—and the other a son thirteen years and one month old, and there exist no previous engagement, little time is lost in clinching the matrimonial bargain. Even if the children have not attained the lawful age, so that they cannot be married at once, still, if the boy be a year or more older than the girl,—say the former six and the latter five,— the bargain is soon struck.

Each then makes a memorandum of the family, name, and residence of the other, with the ages of the boy and girl; and, although years may pass without their hearing from each other, when the children have reached the marriageable age the parents enter into correspondence and fix the wedding-day.

The wedding ceremony always takes place at the residence of the bride's parents. As the intended bride of the son of our host lived in the same town, it happened all the more conveniently for us; and I will now attempt to describe the ceremony as I witnessed it.

At ten o'clock we joined the crowd of invited guests, relatives and others, and the whole company, formed two by two, proceeded to the residence of the bride's parents, all dressed in gala costume as already described, the bridegroom being escorted by his father and his future father-in-law. Arrived at the house, the bridegroom was locked up in a room and left alone to meditate and pray. It should be stated, also, that on this eventful day he is obliged to fast, not having been permitted to taste food since the preceding evening, until the ceremony in the synagogue has been concluded. The bride is kept in seclusion for seven days before the wedding, during which time she is not allowed to see or speak to any man except her father or brother.

We found the house filled with guests, prominent among whom were the relations on both sides, who sometimes on such occasions come from the remotest parts of the country. The men were ranged on one side of the long hall, the women on the other, leaving a space in the centre for the immediate relations of the betrothed pair. At the farther end of the hall, on a slight elevation, was placed a chair covered with richly-embroidered cushions, and behind it stood two young girls about ten or eleven years old, the favorite playmates of the bride.

As soon as order was established, the musicians struck up a march, whereupon the bride made her appearance, advancing through the open space, her mother on her left, and the mother of the bridegroom on her right. She was very young,—seemingly not more than thirteen years of age. She was attired in a close-fitting white muslin dress; and from the top of her head hung a piece of rich velvet about four yards in length, embroidered in gold with cabalistic figures, and which, falling gracefully over her shoulders, formed a sort of mantle, the ends of which were adorned with silver tassels and borne by two of her schoolmates.

To me she looked like a mere child,—as indeed she was. Yet thus early her destiny for life was sealed, and she was assigned the companion at whose side she was to walk until death should separate them, and that companion one whose face she had never yet seen, whose voice she had never heard.

Her countenance was death-like,—her pallor being heightened by contrast with her raven-black hair, of which in a few moments she was to be deprived.

The procession, consisting of her playmates, sisters, cousins, and nearest relations, moved slowly along. When they arrived at the place where stood the chair, she was seated in it, whereupon the music ceased, and from the midst of the company a man stepped forth who, at a later stage of the proceedings, was to enact a part for the general amusement. The clown, as this individual was called, is always present upon occasions like that which I am describing; and his business is to sing comic songs and make the entire assemblage merry with his witticisms. Sometimes, at the weddings of the richer Jews, there are three or four of these clowns.

The clown of the present occasion was a young man of pleasing face, and seemed to be well acquainted with the works of many of the best authors of modern times. He delivered a lecture to the bride, in which he certainly did not play the merry-andrew's part; for he reminded her of the duties inseparable from the state of life which she was about to enter, exhorted her to take leave of her father and mother, brothers and sisters, for that henceforth she would belong to her husband alone, and pointed out the difficulties and dangers that would beset her path. The whole address was recited in verse; and every one present was sensibly affected, the bride and her mother weeping bitterly, and embracing each other as though their separation was to be for eternity. My friend and myself were also not unmoved, but for a very different reason: to us the marriage of two mere children seemed nothing better than barbarism and unworthy the sanction of a civilized people.

While the bride was being thus addressed, the two young girls who stood behind her divested her of the rich velvet cloak, unfastened her hair, and presented to the mother of the bridegroom a silver salver on which was a pair of scissors. The future mother-in-law immediately set to work to cut off the bride's hair; and, as ringlet after ringlet dropped to the floor, we could not repress a feeling of pity at seeing the poor child deprived of one of the most beautiful gifts of nature to her sex. She seemed, however, to be indifferent to every thing except the approaching separation, alternately embracing her mother and wiping away the tears that coursed down her own cheeks.

As soon as the hair had been cut off, a neat little cap, made of tulle blonde, was placed on the bride's head, she was once more invested with the mantle, and all was made ready to resume the procession. When she arrived at the door which led to the street, her future lord and master stood before her, accompanied by his father and the father of the bride. Whether there was any emotion of love in those youthful bosoms I know not; but to me it seemed as if they could look at the whole performance in no other light than that of a comedy in which they were the leading actors. As they met, the gaze of the assembly was upon them; and each stood silent, with eyes downcast, as if ashamed to look at the other. At that moment the youngest sister of the bride, stepping forward, held before her a salver, on which was a white gown of the finest linen, the breast and sleeves of which were adorned with blonde. Taking it from the salver, the bride presented it to her future husband. It was the death-dress, called "Kittel,"—the one the Jew must wear when he takes the vows of matrimony, and that in which he is dressed when giving testimony before a Christian court. It is also the dress worn in the synagogue on the fast-day called *Yom Kippur;* and, finally, in it he is buried when death has removed him from the scenes of earth.

It seems a curious custom thus to attire the Jew in the death-robe on the day which ought to be the happiest of a man's life,—that on which he is united to the being whom he loves above all others,—and thereby remind him of his mortality, knowing as he does that in that very dress he is to be enwrapped when he shall have bid an eternal farewell to the ties and pleasures of this world.

The bridegroom having received this the first gift of his bride, the procession moved on, two by two, until the synagogue was reached. As soon as they had entered, he put the *kittel* on over his other clothes, and added a white cape, which is also a part of the death-dress. Both he and the bride had removed their shoes before entering the temple.

They now advanced to the steps that led to the tabernacle; and the singers *Chason* chanted a psalm appropriate to the occasion. This concluded, the rabbi, or high-priest, made his appearance. He was robed in the peculiar white woollen sheet which every Jew is obliged to wear in the synagogue after he has reached his thirteenth year.

Placing himself in front of the youthful couple, he received thirteen gold pieces from the bridegroom, and, putting them in the bride's hand, pronounced the following words :—" I hereby buy thee with this coin, conformably to the law of Moses," the bridegroom repeating the words after him. After this the rabbi took a glass tumbler, filled it with red wine, pronounced a benediction over it, and placed it to the lips of the bride and the bridegroom in succession, at the same time repeating a prayer. When they had both tasted the wine, he dashed the glass to the floor, shivering it into a thousand pieces, and said, "As the fragments of this glass now broken can never again be united, so shall ye be united never to be broken in two."

The ceremony was now concluded ; and all the relations and friends of the contracting parties came forward with congratulations upon the *Masel tof* (good fortune), after which the whole company returned to the house of the bride's father, to participate in the wedding-feast.

As we had now become deeply interested in the ceremonies, and were desirous to observe the further movements of the happy couple, we accompanied the party, and were so fortunate as to be seated at table directly opposite the child-wife, the object of the day's festivities.

Before the guests sat down, a basin was handed around, into which each had to dip his hand and throw water three times over his finger-ends, while murmuring some sort of prayer; and then each one broke a piece of bread, again repeating a prayer.

During the meal I witnessed another ceremony, which I must here describe. A large table was placed in the centre of the room : this the father of the bride approached, bearing a heavy bag, and counted down upon it, in golden ducats, the dowry of his daughter, taking a receipt for it from the new-made husband and his father.

Immediately after the supper, the clown reappeared, in a fantastic dress, and, placing himself at the centre of the table, requested all who had brought presents for the bride to deliver them to him. This, to the married children, was by far the most interesting part of the ceremony. First in order were announced the gifts of the bridegroom's father and mother, consisting of a dozen silver forks, knives, and spoons; and thus the whole company contributed as they saw proper. My friend and myself, not having been aware of this custom of present-making, had of course come unprepared; but, in order to avoid any semblance of penuriousness, we each sent a ducat to the clown, who announced the amount of our gift in a stentorian voice, probably out of compliment to our liberality. We were told that the wedding-presents at these marriage-suppers not unfrequently amount to more than the dowry.

The festivities were kept up till midnight, when the newly-married couple were escorted by torch-bearers, accompanied with music, to the room set apart for them. When they had entered, the door was locked

from the outside by the clown, who, after a long de-
bate, delivered the key to the bride's mother,—but not
until she had paid a ransom for it.

For three years after the wedding-day the young
folks live with the parents of the bride, who are obliged
to maintain them; then they remove for three additional years to the home of the bridegroom's father.
These six years completed, the married couple are expected to maintain themselves,—generally in some
business established for them by the parents. I have
seen women who at the time they left the parental
roof—that is, at the age of eighteen or nineteen—were
already the mothers of four children. This will explain the multitude of screens we noticed at our tavern,
concealing the rooms occupied by the young married
people and their offspring.

By this rather long digression, which has taken up
more space than I intended, I desire to show that the
custom of marrying girls at the age of from twelve to
thirteen is not peculiar to the Arabs of North Africa,
but may be found in the heart of civilized Europe. I
will now go back to the nomads, taking up the thread
of the narrative at the place where I dropped it.

The girl who served the coffee to me was the youngest
daughter of my host. Her husband was at that time
absent with a caravan. He owned a few camels, with
which he traded between Oran and Morocco, and did
not visit his home more than once or twice a year, even
then remaining but a week or two.

In the tent where I had taken up my abode lived
the great-grandfather of the family, a venerable Arab,
about eighty years of age. He seemed quite happy
and contented; and when I asked him how he passed

his time, he replied that he spent it in meditating on the life to come, and on the joys that awaited him in the Paradise of Mohammed.

Among these people, the aged never become so dull and infirm as they do with us. Generally, their bodily agility and freshness remain apparently unimpaired until within a few days before death, which seems to come upon them almost without warning. To the close of his life, the Arab exults in the open air. The cold night-air, the rain and storm, have no terrors for him; but, instead, as he grows older he learns more and more to delight in the scenes of nature. While the young man is safely ensconced in his comfortable tent, the old patriarch will sit outside all night to enjoy the moonlight. When the elements are fiercely battling, when all nature seems to be disturbed, and every living being but himself has sought shelter, he, seated on a rock or under some old palm or olive tree, views with feelings of delight the strife that is going on. When his camelhair abode is shaken by the hurricane, when the thunder peals in terrific volleys, and its reverberations are echoed by the crags and precipices of the Atlas, then does the spirit of the old man exult in the majesty of Allah, his God and the God of his prophet, and his lips move in heartfelt devotion.

As he feels his end drawing near, he becomes more thoughtful and silent. He has no fear of death, but rather yearns for it, looks forward to its coming with the feeling experienced by those who are awaiting the moment that shall bring with it the full fruition of the heart's desire.

Very few Arabs, at least as compared with Europeans, die of disease. Death with them seems to be a sudden crisis, the result of a pause in the circulation of the blood through sheer weakness, the exhaustion of the powers of the machine called the body; and life is extinguished without the agony that seems to us the inseparable companion of the parting hour.

When it is certain that the hour of death is at hand, the old man is carried in the arms of his sons and grandsons and placed in front of the tent, where he is laid on a bed of sheepskins and palm-leaf mats; and there, with his face turned towards the rising sun in the direction of the *Kaaba* and the tomb of Mohammed, he peacefully closes his eyes, in the full confidence which all the faithful enjoy that he is about to enter that Paradise, full of unutterable delights, of which he learned to dream when but a child, and the vision of which in after-years, as he crossed the burning sands of the Desert or pursued the game in the wild fastnesses of the Atlas, seemed even brighter than it had appeared in the thoughtless days of boyhood. Such is the parting hour of the aged Arab, free from all that makes death terrible to the cultivated man of the West.

All his nearest of kin gather around him, and wait in solemn silence until the last breath is gasped out. Then they give full vent to their grief. The females weep and shriek; while the marabout invokes Allah and prays to Mohammed to open to the departed the doors of Paradise.

The grief of the Arab for his departed relative is deep and unaffected. He loves his parents when living, and after their death he fondly cherishes their memory. The most beautiful spot he can find is selected as their last resting-place:—in the north, among the romantic dells of the Atlas; in the oases, near some brook, and surrounded by palm-trees. Three stones, without inscription or ornament, mark the grave, which are kissed and moistened with tears whenever the survivors visit the place.

The city of Algiers has a beautiful cemetery, the sepulchral monuments in which are very fine. During my stay in that city my attention was called to the tomb of the five murdered Deys, who perished in the year 1779, when the Janizaries were divided into two factions of equal strength and could not agree in the selection of a ruler.

As soon as a candidate of one party was clad in the imperial robes, the opposing party put him to death, and set their own favorite on the throne, who in his turn was immediately murdered by the first party. Again and again was the bloody scene re-enacted during the day, until five unfortunates had paid for their brief elevation with their lives; and at last the contending factions, weary of fighting, decided upon a curious way of settling the question of successorship. It was agreed that the officers of both sides should go in a body to the grand mosque, and the first Turk whom they should chance to see coming out of it was to be the Dey.

It so happened that the lot fell upon a cobbler, who, aware of the summary fate of his predecessors, was greatly alarmed when he heard himself hailed by the Janizaries as Dey, and loudly asseverated his incapacity and his unworthiness of the office. His remonstrances availed him nothing, however: he was immediately clad in the robes of state and seated upon the red velvet cushion, while the muezzins proclaimed to the inhabitants that a ruler had been appointed.

This chance selection, nevertheless, turned out to be

a happy one. The cobbler ruled with wisdom and justice, and proved to be one of the best Deys Algiers had ever possessed. He caused his five slaughtered predecessors to be buried close to each other, and erected to their memory five monuments, in the shape of five minarets of oblong, slender form, richly decorated with marble and porcelain. These are still in existence; but the French soldiery have sacrilegiously defaced them.

After seeing every thing of interest in the Arab village, I bade farewell to my host, with expressions of the most heartfelt gratitude for his kindness, and returned to Oran.

On my arrival at the city, I was surprised to hear a loud cannonading. I inquired the cause, and was told that it denoted the beginning of the *Ramadan,* the great Mohammedan fast, which is always signalized by a salvo of one hundred and one guns, the expense of which is levied on the Mohammedan population at the rate of one *duro* (four shillings) for each gun.

Upon the cessation of the firing, the signal lamps on the balconies of the mosque-steeple were lighted, with brilliant effect. In the centre of this luminous circle stood the muezzin in holiday costume, who, hoisting the white flag, proclaimed the fast of Allah and summoned the faithful to prayer and worship. Not a single believer in Mohammed, in any of the cities of Algeria, would refuse to obey the call of the muezzin as he announces the beginning of the Ramadan.

All the mosques of Oran were filled with Mussulmans during the continuance of this fast; and, as I had nothing to occupy my attention particularly, I visited one of them, that I might witness the ceremony, which

I was aware differed from that used on ordinary occasions.

The interior architecture of these mosques is everywhere the same,—the only difference being in size or in richness of materials, according to the population and wealth of the place where they are situated. On the present occasion, the interior colonnade of the one I visited was resplendent with the light of what seemed almost an infinite number of lamps. In the recess of the sanctuary stood the *Mufti-el-Hanefi*, or *Sheikh-el-Islam*, with the Koran open before him, from which he read some chapters, and then, bowing his head and praying in a low tone, waited until the assembly should be sufficiently large to warrant his beginning the ceremony of the day.

The greater number of the worshippers stood in long rows, their faces turned towards the niche; but some were sitting cross-legged, as dumb and motionless as though they had suddenly turned to marble. All at once the voice of the priest was heard throughout the temple, repeating prayers that resembled somewhat the litany of the Roman Catholic Church. These concluded, he read several chapters from the Koran, intermingling his readings with piercing lamentations, which sounded like the agonized cries of a suffering man rather than the promptings of devotion. The burden of the Ramadan prayer is the lowliest self-abasement in the presence of a stern and all-powerful Deity. The moaning utterances of the mufti soon merged into a mournful song, and, after this had continued for a little while, his voice sank by gentle cadences until it died away in silence.

During all this time the congregation had been seized

with what appeared to me like convulsive fits, which seemed to increase or diminish in force as the mufti's voice rose or fell. They threw themselves head-foremost on the carpet, bowed, kneeled, rose again,—in short, were so extravagant in their demonstrations that I could easily have imagined myself an on-looker at some acrobatic exhibition. All their motions were characterized by system and regularity; and, as the steps of the ballet-dancer are guided by the music, so did the convulsions of the faithful on this occasion appear to be directed by the voice of the mufti.

It looked strange to see the proud, overbearing Mohammedan, who ordinarily will not bow his head for any earthly power, and who, even if condemned to death, marches with erect and undaunted mien, thus prostrated in abject humiliation at the feet of Allah, trembling with the consciousness of moral uncleanness.

In the mosque there are no distinctions of rank or race. On this occasion Moors, Turks, Arabs, Koloughs, Kabyls, negroes, and Biskaris were all intermingled,— the Turk, in his gaudy dress, by the side of the ragged and beggarly Biskari,—the pale, handsome-featured Moor next to the malformed, hideous, apelike negro of Soudan,—all worshipping Allah with the selfsame appearance of pious devotion.

The Mohammedan, like the Roman Catholic, invariably has a rosary twined around his hands when he prays. The same custom obtains among the Buddhists. The people use them only in the mosque, while at prayer; but the muftis and marabouts constantly wear them around their necks, in token of their superior piety. In some parts of Algeria these rosaries are made of the seeds of the dwarf palm (*Chamærops humilis*).

Abd-el-Kader, when a prisoner in France, was never seen in public without a rosary in his hand. He was renowned among his countrymen for his devotion to the faith. Being the son of a marabout,—Sidi Mahiddin, — he had in early life been destined to the vocation of priest; and not until he was placed at the head of the horsemen of his tribe to withstand the foreign invader did he relinquish it for that of the warrior.

After the force of the convulsions had passed away, the devotees remained motionless for some minutes, mumbling a short prayer, with their heads bowed on their breasts. They then bade adieu to the sacred place, and, entering the courts, among the orange-groves of which are the fountains of consecrated water, washed their hands and feet, put on their sandals, and departed.

Once out of the mosque, the quondam worshipper soon sheds his thin covering of piety. The Moor goes back to his beautiful residence, where his sultana awaits his coming; the Arab returns to his *jubar*, the Bedouin to his tent in the plains, the Kabyl to his mud hut in the mountains; and should an opportunity for plunder present itself to the latter, on his way home, he is not long in availing himself of it, even though the victim be a co-religionist; while the life of any unlucky Christian whom he might happen to meet in a lonely spot would not be worth a great deal.

The fast of Ramadan lasts for thirty days. During the whole time the Mohammedan observes a rigid abstinence from sunrise till sunset; but as soon as the report of the cannon announces the close of the day, he sits down to the meal which has been made ready in anticipation, and gratifies his sharpened appetite to the full, winding up the evening with music, dancing, theatrical performances, and all sorts of games.

During the nights of the Ramadan the coffee-houses are the great centres of attraction, at each of which a kind of masquerade is to be witnessed, such as is common in the Roman Catholic countries of Europe during the Carnival.

At the close of the Ramadan begins the *Bairam*, the feast of joy and reconciliation,—as Easter follows Lent in the Christian world. During its continuance bands of negro minstrels throng the streets, filling the air with their deafening music, and every one whom they meet becomes tributary to the amount of one penny, or, if he refuses, gets considerably more than a pennyworth of molestation. At these times the natives are to be seen clad in their best attire; and even the women are then often beheld in the streets,—always, however, with the abominable veil. The little boys sprinkle rose-water on the passers-by,—especially on the Europeans; and the Mussulmans kiss each other on the shoulder.

On the evening of the first day of the Ramadan I visited some other mosques, where I found the ceremonies precisely like those I have already described. Each of these had its fountain of sacred water, wherein the Mussulman washes his face, hands, and feet with the most scrupulous care every time he enters or departs from the mosque. The floors are covered with fine velvet carpet, that nearest the niche where the mufti officiates being of surpassing richness in color and texture.

Although in Oran the Mussulmans do not fraternize with the Europeans, as they do in Algiers, the prejudice against Christians is far from being so marked as in many of the petty towns of the interior. The entrance of an infidel into a mosque no longer excites the horror that it did in bygone days; and I passed in and out of the Mohammedan temples as freely as though they had been churches of my own faith,—except that I had to take off my shoes at the door, since the sacred carpet is not to be trodden by any but uncovered feet.

In the interior towns, however, no such tolerance exists; for only sixteen years ago, if a Christian ventured to enter a mosque in any of these places, the unlucky trespasser was put to death, and the floor of the mosque was carefully washed and its walls freshly painted, to remove the pollution inseparable from the presence of an unbeliever.

Here again we may find a parallel in the Christian world. A fanaticism quite as fierce in its spirit as that of the half-civilized Algerines existed, no farther back than 1861, among the inmates of the cloisters and convents of Mexico. No woman was allowed to enter a cloister of the monks; but if, by some unlucky chance, one of the despised sex gained admittance, it became necessary to consecrate the halls anew, and by the burning of incense and the chanting of prayers to drive away the foul spirit that had come among them in the form of a woman.

And so with the convents of the nuns. If a man intruded upon the sacred precincts, either by accident or design, the inmates were even more rigorous in their measures of purification than the monks in the like contingency.

An amusing illustration of this was given in what took place in one of the nunneries of the city of Mexico.

The story was told to me by the involuntary cause of contamination himself.

It was when the French troops were approaching the capital, and the so-called Liberal ‚Government was busily engaged in devising sham measures of defence. Special contributions—matters of very frequent occurrence, by the way, in unhappy Mexico—were levied on all residents, foreigners as well as citizens, to assist in defraying the expenses of the war, the government declaring that the lives and property of all belonged to the nation, and must be at its disposal in case of need.

The members of a few of the still existing convents were the first on whom heavy contributions were levied, since it was believed that they were in possession of a great deal of hidden treasure, and since also less resistance was likely to be encountered than from ordinary citizens; for in cases of this kind the threat was always held out that if they refused to comply with the government's demands they would be driven from their home, their movable property would be confiscated, and, worst of all, the ground on which stood their holy abode would be parcelled out into city lots. It was very rarely necessary, therefore, to call twice on the nuns on an errand like this.

The abbess of the convent of La Encarnacion—the wealthiest in the city—received one morning an unwelcome invitation from the secretary of the state treasury to pay, within twenty-four hours, a contribution of twenty-five thousand dollars towards the defence of the country. This invitation, on the outside of which was written, in large letters, the word "Urgent," was handed in through a lattice window in the portcress's cell, and the next instant it lay on the table of the most reverend Mother Maria de Jesus, abbess of the ancient and wealthy convent of La Encarnacion. With trembling hands she unfolded the paper, and as soon as she had read it she called a council of the sisters. They soon determined on the course to be pursued. Rather than subject themselves to prosecution by a refusal to comply with the politely-expressed wish of the authorities, they resolved to pay the money, yielding with the best possible grace what would otherwise be taken by force; and a note was dispatched to a Mr. D——, the agent in the city of Mexico of a well-known English banking-house, begging him to come forthwith to the nunnery on important business.

It is an invariable rule in all the convents—and it was enforced with extreme rigor in La Encarnacion —that no man can be admitted within their sacred precincts except the father confessor, or, in cases of urgency, the doctor; and the latter is almost always an old man of unblemished character and undoubted devotion to the Church.

At the same time that the message was dispatched to the man of finances, another was sent to the doctor, whose presence was needed at once, one of the nuns being at that moment at the point of death. Confusion and distress reigned throughout the sisterhood, for the dying nun was beloved of all; and the porteress was directed to conduct the doctor to the cell of the sufferer as soon as he arrived. This porteress was a lay sister, and, having been but a short time an inmate of the convent, had never seen the doctor, and of course did not know him.

After a brief interval, the money-agent presented himself at the gate. The bell was rung; and the por-

teress, making sure that it was the doctor, ushered the
visitor into the hall, and bade him follow her.

The nuns were by this time all gathered round the
bed of the sufferer, waiting anxiously for the coming
of the physician.

As Mr. D—— followed his guide through the long
corridors of the convent, he could not help wondering
at so unusual a proceeding; but, thinking that perhaps
the urgency of the business upon which he had been
summoned was the occasion of this departure from
long-established custom,. he asked no questions.

On went the porteress at her swiftest pace, our friend
having as much as he could do to keep up with her,
until she stopped before the sick-room. The door being
opened, the nuns beheld a good-looking young man, one
whose face they had never seen before, and, screaming,
they fled in all directions, leaving the stranger alone with
the dying nun.

The outcry of the startled sisters was heard by the
abbess, who, on inquiring what terrible misfortune had
befallen them, was horrified by the intelligence that a
young and strange man had violated by his presence
the sanctity of their abode. Bewildered, she went back
to her own cell with some of the frightened sisters, to
hold a brief consultation with them; and they soon
arrived at the conclusion that the intruder was one of
the Government officials, come to enforce the speedy
payment of the contribution that had been levied upon
them. The alarm-bell was sounded, the porteress and
the lay sisters were summoned, and a messenger was
sent to the supposed official, to ascertain the exact
nature of his errand.

In the mean time, Mr. D—— was in sore perplexity.

The screams of the nuns, together with their precipi-
tate flight from the room, had astonished and somewhat
bewildered him; and he was trying to collect his scattered thoughts, so as to account for the odd manner in
which he had been received, when the lay sister appeared,
with the message of the abbess. Seeing now that there
must be some mistake, he sent his *carte de visite* to the
abbess, and waited in the corridor for her reply.

When the abbess read the name of Mr. D——, she
understood at once the origin of the trouble,—the ignorance on the part of the porteress concerning the physician of the convent. She immediately ordered all the
nuns to retire to their cells, while two of the oldest lay
sisters were to blindfold Mr. D—— and conduct him
to the reception-room, where she would give him an
interview.

To the proposition of blindfolding Mr. D—— gave
a somewhat reluctant assent; but, the bandage not being
put on very tightly, he was able to see that many of
the nuns were slyly peeping from their cells, to get a
glimpse of the handsome young stranger whose presence
had caused such a fluttering in their peaceful nest.

As soon as he arrived in presence of the abbess, his
eyes were unbandaged, and, after mutual apologies and
explanations, the business which had brought him to
the convent was satisfactorily transacted.

He had hardly taken his leave, however, when the
abbess dispatched a messenger to the archbishop, to
ascertain the most effectual method of averting the evil
consequences of the horrible desecration to which the
convent had been subjected. The archbishop, who,
despite his ecclesiastical robes, was a man of the world,
directed the frightened women to offer up an additional

15

Ave Maria for three consecutive days, to abstain from flesh-meat the same length of time, to have the corridor scrupulously cleansed, and to burn incense three times a day in the polluted corridors and cell,—this also to continue for three days.

In this instance the contamination was considered particularly serious, because the innocent cause of it was an Israelite.

When Mr. D—— sent to the convent the much-needed twenty-five thousand dollars, he could not but wonder whether it would be necessary to fumigate the money, coming as it did from the hands of one so utterly unclean, before it could be allowed to enter the sacred precincts.

In the above-narrated incident we have an exemplification of a fanaticism quite as ridiculous as that of the fiercest Mohammedan on earth; nor would there be any difficulty in adducing instances of the operation of the same spirit in almost any country of Christendom.

In Algiers and the other principal cities of the French possessions in Africa, the intercourse between the European and the infidel, under circumstances very different from those of former times, aided also, perhaps, by the powerful repressing arm of the French government, has tended to soften the antagonisms of religion, and the Mohammedans no longer consider a mosque defiled should a Christian chance to enter it.

During the intensely hot weather which prevails in that country, the mosques are agreeable places of resort for the European who is in search of some cool spot where he may rest for an hour or two. Whenever I visited a mosque during my stay there, it was as much with the purpose of escaping the oppressive heat, as from any other cause. At the same time, I often found food for study in them, while watching the faces of the worshippers, either singly in the daytime or in groups at evening prayers. On one occasion I was particularly impressed by the appearance of a melancholy-looking, silver-haired old Moor, who seemed to be yearning for the promised blessings, while beside him was his grandchild or great-grandchild, a beautiful, rosy-cheeked little fellow, in whose heart—to judge from his face—fanaticism had not yet taken root. Often, too, might the devotees be seen listlessly wandering through the orange groves in the inner courts, lulled into revery by the harmonious cadences of the rippling fountains.

Among the mosques at Oran—which, by the way, are far from being so grand, either in architecture or decoration, as those of Algiers—is one that contains the remains of some peculiarly holy marabout. It is opened once a year to a few privileged ones among the faithful; at all other times it is kept locked. Of course I had no opportunity of visiting it.

Another mosque that is constantly kept closed is the one that stands near the gate of Bab-a-Tun, at Algiers. Into this no one can gain admittance; but the curious traveller, as well as the devout follower of the Prophet, is permitted to gaze at the interior through a grated hole, by which means a faint idea of its magnificence may be obtained. The walls, ceilings, and floor are covered with rich velvet embroidered in gold with figures of flowers and with inscriptions from the Koran. Above the niche are various sculptured symbolic figures, of the finest white marble; while in the niche itself is an altar of the same material, on which rests a marble sarcophagus, overhung with a great number of richly-embroidered flags of curious shape.

This is the mausoleum of the renowned prince of the corsair republic, Khair-ed-Deen Barbarossa, who defeated the expedition of Charles V. in the year 1541. He died in 1546.

Finding nothing further in Oran to engage my attention, I determined to proceed to Tlemcen. I accordingly secured a seat in the post-chaise that runs daily between the two places, and the next morning at three o'clock I squeezed myself in between a Moor on one side and a stout Frenchwoman on the other, and off we started.

This kind of travel reminds me of that in vogue in Mexico,—with the sole difference that there the vehicles are of American manufacture and therefore commodious, while those that run between Oran and Tlemcen are so constructed—or at least they were at the time of my visit—that when the coach has its complement the passengers are packed in like sardines, without room to move. Woe betide the unlucky traveller in one of these conveyances who is afflicted with tender feet! for sitting opposite to him are three fellow-travellers, and considerable ingenuity is required to arrange the extremities so that no sudden movement of the vehicle may bring the heel of his opposite neighbor into disagreeable contact with his own sensitive toes.

At Miserghin, not far from Oran, is a ruined building that was formerly a country palace of the Deys of Oran. What most interested me about it was the court of lions. At the period of my visit there still remained five of these animals. I was informed that originally they numbered twenty-five, but that all except the five then alive had been killed by order of the French commander, on account of the expense of feeding them.

Here for the first time I met with the ostrich. As I purpose giving a full description of this bird in the account of my travels in the Sahara, where I saw them in flocks, I shall say nothing about them here. Those kept at Miserghin were very wretched specimens. This bird, like the Arab, flourishes nowhere but on the broad sandy plains where it is free from the trammels of man : in captivity it loses the greater part of its beauty and majestic bearing.

After leaving Miserghin the stage passes along the western shore of the great Sebkah, the lake whose waters supply the inhabitants of the country, far and wide, with salt.

Perhaps some of my readers will be amused at the comparisons I draw between the lower order of Arabs and the half-civilized Indian of Mexico. The parallel, nevertheless, holds good in all points but one; and that is, that, with but few exceptions, the Mexican Indian is of mongrel breed, having the blood of the Spaniard or the negro in his veins, while the Arab has preserved for centuries the type and purity of his race. The outer covering of the Arab, called the *burnus*, is the *jorongo* of the Mexican Indian, worn merely in a different way. The domestic utensils in the tent of the one are precisely similar to those in the cane hut of the other. The Arab *sheik* in the *jugar* is the exact equivalent of the Mexican *caizig* in his *pueblo*. The tattooed Arab woman can claim sisterhood, in habits and appearance, with the Indian woman of Mexico. The Mexican crossbreed is treacherous and thievish, and his heart is filled with hatred of the foreigners; the same qualities characterize the Arab. The mode of living, habits, and customs of the two races are almost exactly alike; and both manifest the same inveterate hostility to any innovation upon the customs of their ancestors, and the same deep-rooted aversion to whatever savors of improvement.

The Arab mode of gathering salt from the Sebkah is exactly similar to that of the Indians near the Lake of Tezcuco in Mexico. The waters of both these lakes are surcharged with salt; but neither the Arab nor the Indian has ever attempted to improve upon the primitive mode of extracting it as handed down from his forefathers. In both instances the water is evaporated by the heat of the sun, and the crystallized salt is then collected and taken to market.

I cannot help giving in this place a striking illustration of the excessive indolence of the Mexican in the *tierra caliente*. His daily food consists of a sort of dried pancake, called *tortilla*, and of beans stewed with lard and spiced with *chile*. Rarely does he taste flesh, unless when he happens to obtain a little by hunting. On his wife devolves the task of preparing his meals, while he, as occasion requires, procures the requisite wood and water in the following ingeniously lazy way. Suspending across the back of his mule a couple of earthen jars, he mounts, and proceeds at a leisurely pace to the nearest river, where he drives the animal into the water until he reaches a depth sufficient to fill the jars. This done, he rides up to some dried trunk or branch of a fallen tree, ties his lasso around it, secures the lasso to the pommel of his saddle, and forthwith proceeds to his dwelling, supplied with wood and water without having found it necessary to get off his mule.

A degree of laziness, this, which one sometimes finds paralleled among the lower order of Arabs.

When the post-chaise arrived at the Isser, where a fresh relay of horses was taken, I determined to let it go on without me, and to procure a guide and a horse and proceed in that manner to Tlemcen.

The relays along this route are kept by Arabs; and a rougher-looking set of fellows I never beheld. The post-chaise had hardly disappeared in the distance, when I repented very heartily of my rashness in abandoning it, despite its inconveniences; for the faces of the men around me filled me with horror. They were so covered with vermin that I could not bear to go near them; and their scowling, malignant countenances, begrimed with filth, had by no means a reassuring effect upon my disturbed nervous system.

I began to be conscious of having placed myself in a very awkward predicament; but, there being now no alternative, I resolved to put the best possible face on the matter, and tried to compose myself into a feeling of security. To gain the good will of the Arabs, I offered them tobacco with every appearance of good-fellowship; but my bounty was accepted without a single word of thanks. There they sat in ominous silence, merely nodding in answer to my smiling observations and questions; and very soon the conviction forced itself upon me that their gloomy reserve betokened no good to me. I asked for the promised horse and guide, but was told that the former was out at pasture and had first to be caught, while the latter had not yet arrived from a neighboring village, to which he had been sent on an errand. On hearing this, I began to reflect seriously on my prospect for reaching Tlemcen at all. I would have been glad to be allowed to pursue my way on foot; but it was evident that my every movement was closely watched by the ill-looking scoundrels who surrounded me. Thinking that the best plan for my personal safety was to betray no apprehension of evil, and to act as coolly as though I were among friends, I lit a cigar, at the same time taking from my pocket a neat little six-shooter, which I carefully inspected as if to be certain that it would not fail me in an emergency, watching all the while the effect of this proceeding on the faces of the Arabs.

Among the agreeable little party into whose company I had fallen was one young fellow whose muscular and symmetrical frame and regular features would have fitted him to be a model for a sculptor. To make him presentable in civilized society, however, it would have been necessary to subject him to the purifying influences of a twice-repeated Russian hot-water and vapor bath. He was apparently not more than twenty-four years old, was tall and strongly-built, and the expression of his face was that of a fierce determination to carry out his designs, whether for good or for evil. By this individual, it appeared to me, I was most closely watched. Not a muscle of his face quivered as he bent his cold, stern gaze upon me, his fiery dark eyes seeming to fix me to the spot as if by a baleful magnetism.

Having satisfied myself as to the condition of my revolver, I laid it down beside me, and took out its companion, as if to examine it also, but really in the hope that the sight of my weapons would cause my friends to pause and calculate the risk that would be incurred in attacking me. No sooner, however, had I exhibited the second revolver, than the young Arab whom I have described, with one bound, seized the one which lay at my side, almost before I was aware of the movement; and the next instant he was some twenty paces off. There he stood like a statue, his fiery gaze fixed on me as if defying me to reclaim my property. The action was so sudden, in so unexpected a manner had the fellow's evil intent taken shape, that for a few minutes I was thunderstruck. I looked at his companions, in mute inquiry as to the meaning of this proceeding; but they remained silent and unconcerned, as if what had happened had been well understood between them beforehand. Seeing that no assistance was to be expected in that quarter, I rose from my seat and asked the robber to restore the weapon; but he made so defiant a gesture that I did not think it prudent to approach him. However, summoning up my courage, which for an instant had failed me, unnerved as I was by the sinister looks of the party and the boldness of the theft, I cocked my second revolver, and advanced towards him. Simultaneously my adversary cocked the stolen weapon, and, without moving from his position, waited until I was within a few paces of him; then, raising the revolver, he fired. Whether he intentionally missed me or not, I cannot say; but the ball whistled harmlessly past me, though it sounded very disagreeably near. I halted at the report; whereupon he said, "I do not intend to kill you. All I want is this weapon: you have two, and can therefore afford to give away one. I warn you, however, not to fire; for, by Allah and his prophet, I will not spare you if you show the slightest intention of hurting me."

Alone as I was among these villains, and completely

in their power, discretion seemed by far the better part
of valor, and I signified my acquiescence in his demand
with all the grace I could muster under the circumstances, remarking that there was no occasion for any
difficulty between us, since if he had asked for the
weapon I would willingly have given it to him. I
thought to gain the good will and friendly offices of
the whole band by this affectation of generosity, but
soon found I had committed a blunder more egregious
even than that of carelessly laying the first revolver by
my side; for scarcely had I uttered the words when
another ruffian stepped up to me and, in the rudest
manner imaginable, demanded the pistol I had in my
hand.

This, I thought, was carrying the matter a little too
far. There seemed, however, to be no alternative.
Resistance could avail but little, since if they had
wished to kill me they had only to make use of their
long-barrelled guns that were stacked in one corner.
Nevertheless, I ventured to expostulate, telling them
that I could not travel if destitute of the means of defence. To this they replied that I need not stand in
any fear of attack on the road, since the Arabs were all
honest. As I had just had a very practical demonstra-
tion of the nature of their honesty, I failed to see why
I should give up my remaining weapon, and signified
my unwillingness as forcibly as I dared; but instantly
my arms were grasped from behind, and in less time
than it takes to tell the story I was absolutely defenceless. Here, then, I stood, far removed from civilized
men, alone among a band of heartless robbers, who
had despoiled me of the first articles of value they had
laid their eyes on, and yet had the effrontery to style

themselves honest. I suppose they based their claim to honesty on their willingness to spare my life, that not being worth the taking; but they certainly would not have hesitated to strip the clothes off my back had the fancy seized them.

Seeing with what perfect ease they could deprive me of my property, they now became somewhat communicative, and, observing that I had a tolerable stock of cigars, they expressed a wish to possess them, remarking that two or three would be enough for my use until I arrived at Tlemcen, while they had no opportunity to get such good ones. Their wishes being commands, I relinquished my cigars, wondering what would be the next article to disappear.

I had by this time, as the reader will have no trouble in believing, become very anxious to proceed on my journey; and I once more inquired for the promised horse and guide. They now told me I could be supplied immediately, provided I paid the duros in advance. Warned by my previous experience to avoid any thing like display, I answered that it was impossible for me to pay until my arrival at Tlemcen, as I had no money with me, but simply a written order. Either they did not believe me, or they wished to make use of the order; for they instantly asked me to show it to them. I happened to have in my pocket a hotel-bill in French, partly printed and partly written; and this I handed to them with all imaginable sang-froid. It passed from hand to hand, until all seemed convinced of its genuineness: very fortunately for me, however, my friends knew about as much of the French language as a Hottentot does of Greek. After they had scrutinized it to their hearts' content, they informed me, to my no small discomfiture, that I would have to remain with them over-night, it being impossible to get a horse then, much less a guide. To this proposition I flatly refused assent; for I was now fully convinced that their object was to plunder me during the night. I told them I was determined to set out at once on foot for Tlemcen, for that it was essential that I should reach that place before dark. Finding me bent upon going, they endeavored to excite my fears by telling me that I might be so unfortunate as to fall into the hands of the Ouled-ben-Youssouf tribe, the inveterate enemies of the Christians, and that in that case I would pay for my rashness with my life. All this had a strange sound from the lips of men who a few minutes previous had told me I needed no fire-arms on the road, because the Arabs were so exceedingly honest.

My situation at this moment was well calculated to check the spirit of adventure which had brought me into this out-of-the-way part of the world and thrown me into such undesirable company. Adventures are all very well after they are over and nothing remains to be done but narrate them to one's friends or commit them to paper; but to be the chief actor, and find one's self in a position similar to mine among these heathen robbers, eliminates the romance pretty effectually at the time, however it may be in the retrospect.

In spite of their dissuasions, I made up my mind to start at once, in the face of the prospect of falling into the hands of Arabs who laid no claim whatever to honesty. Although they saw I was thoroughly in earnest, they showed no disposition to put any obstacle in my way; and I set out, heartily glad to get away from them. The road leading from the station in the direction of Tlemcen ran in a nearly straight line for a couple of miles; and, for a long time, whenever I looked back I could see the "honest" fellows, still seated on the spot where I had parted from them. This inspired me with some degree of confidence, and I pushed on with all the energy I could muster, not knowing at what minute the whim might seize them to make me a target on which to test the range of my lost six-shooters.

After I had travelled a considerable distance, the road diverged, and ran through a densely-wooded country. Here I came to a halt; for the anxieties of the last few hours had greatly disturbed my mind, the perspiration was dripping from my face, and my feet refused to carry me any farther. Seating myself on a rock, I began to ponder my situation. The prospect was certainly rather gloomy; for I had not the slightest idea of the distance to the next station, having entirely forgotten, in my haste to get away from the delectable company I had left, to make inquiries on that point. There was nothing for it but to make up my mind to encounter the worst. Sitting there in that lonely spot, heart-sore and foot-sore, earnest indeed were the resolutions I made to abandon all idea of travelling in uncivilized countries, once I got out of my present difficulties. How to extricate myself from them, however, happened just then to be a difficult problem. I deliberated for some time, endeavoring to determine which was the worse alternative,—to spend the night in the open air and in solitude in a country so wild as this, or to retrace my steps and solicit the hospitality of the scoundrelly Arabs until the morning.

From where I sat I could see the gigantic Atlas in

the distance, its peaks seeming to tower to the heavens. The country around was densely wooded, with a barren spot here and there; and vainly did I try to discover a sign of human habitation. The road before me, I knew, led to Tlemcen; but it would have been impossible for me to reach that place before dark, even had I not been already exhausted. It would, at the same time, be madness to expose myself during the night with the heavens for my tent and the earth for my couch, as I had so often done on former occasions; for I was aware that that section of country swarmed with ferocious beasts of prey. While thus painfully cogitating, I heard a rustling in the woods behind me, and, turning round, beheld the fellow who had robbed me of my second revolver. I immediately suspected that this was the precursor of some new trouble; but the next instant I was agreeably undeceived, for he held out to me the hotel-bill which I had left behind me, and which, being of no use to them, the "honest" Arabs had thus sent to me. I took it from him with many thanks; and I was just about telling him that I would go back and spend the night with his people, when suddenly my first despoiler also came upon the scene. I now felt certain that their designs were evil, and in an instant lost the confidence with which I had been inspired by the apparent friendliness that had prompted the return of the hotel-bill. Nor did I have long to wait for the confirmation of my fears. Without any attempt at parley, one of them seized the leather belt which I wore around my waist, while the other clasped me in his herculean arms, and in an instant I was deprived of all my money. They then disappeared as suddenly as they had come, and once more I was alone, grieving less over the loss of my belt and its contents than over the prospect of having to pass the night in a thick forest without the slightest means of defence against the attacks of the wild animals that infested it. The opportunity of seeking shelter among the Arabs had vanished with the departure of my visitors; and the only course open to me now was to proceed on my journey as long as my strength held out, and then pass the night in a tree. The constant dread of falling into the clutches of some savage beast, added to the depression of my spirits, kept me from making very rapid progress; and, besides, darkness was rapidly closing in upon me, rendering it impossible to be certain in what direction I was moving. I had already travelled, as nearly as I could estimate, about eight miles; and, although I believed that half that distance farther on I should find the next relay, my overpowering fatigue, my faintness from hunger (I had tasted nothing whatever since the morning), and the darkness, soon compelled me to stop and devise some means of shelter. For this purpose I carefully selected a tree whose stout branches and thick foliage would provide me with a place of rest and security. Clambering up its trunk, I settled myself in the most comfortable spot I could find, where I might stretch my aching limbs; and, in order to guard against falling in case I should be overcome by sleep, I made myself fast to the bough on which I sat, by means of my cravat and handkerchief, at the same time commending soul and body to Him who preserved Daniel unscathed in the lions' den.

I soon fell into a profound slumber, utterly exhausted as I was by fatigue and mental anxiety. When I awoke the next morning, the sun was high above the horizon. I looked around, bewildered; for my mind had not entirely recovered from the rude shocks of the previous day. The fancy seized me that my spirit had departed, and was now hovering near its earthly habitation. I imagined I was in the antechamber of purgatory; for around me were the forms of what seemed countless demons, gnashing their teeth and fixing upon me their fierce gaze, accompanying it with unutterably discordant yells and screeches. I expected every moment to see the furnace of torments, with its attendant fiends. I moved my legs and arms, half doubting whether I were still in the flesh; but, finding myself secured to the tree as I had arranged it the preceding evening, I became convinced that I was as yet in the land of realities. I then took a general survey of my situation; and if it were not that Professor Du Chaillu has anticipated me, I would lay claim to the honor of being the first European discoverer of the fierce gorilla; for to my excited imagination the hideous faces around me belonged to a race of monkeys of gigantic size.

I do not wish to excite the nervous system of my reader, — especially if of the gentler sex, — nor do I purpose to give interest to my narrative by drawing upon my imagination; and, in fact, words would fail to describe the horror I experienced as the hopelessness of my situation burst full upon me.

I knew not how to act. I feared that an attempt to descend from my perch would be the signal for a general attack: yet it was impossible for me to remain much longer where I was, for I had had nothing to eat for twenty-four hours, and the pangs of hunger were growing intolerable. I quietly watched the enemy, every instant becoming more fully impressed with the extent of the danger that threatened me. I firmly believe that the monkeys held a council of war, to settle the point whether I was one of their own species who had come from some distant land, or a bold intruder upon their forest sanctuary.

How bitterly did I then regret my want of familiarity with Adelung, and my ignorance of the monkey language! for the noise they made was sufficient to acquaint me with their intentions, had I possessed the faculty of interpreting their articulations.

As soon as I had unbound myself, I began to move, whereupon the whole host of monkeys did the same; and I expected momentarily to hear the word of command, and to be set upon by the hideous troop. To my great surprise and joy, however, the movement was not towards me. With a simultaneous rush they abandoned their positions behind the different branches, and went farther into the forest. Was this merely a strategic retreat to obtain reinforcements? I could not tell: enough, for the present, that the enemy had disappeared. I could now see no living thing except a few birds of brilliant plumage that flew from tree to tree, pursued by one of the eagles which abound in this part of the country.

Not being able to think myself entirely secure as yet, I preferred to maintain my position in the tree rather than expose myself on the public road. I therefore remained for some time where I was, until, to my exceeding delight, I heard the noise of an approaching vehicle. Soon the stage-coach that leaves Oran every morning for Tlemcen made its appearance, and, hailing it with all the power of my lungs, I succeeded in halt-

16*

ing it near the tree upon which I was perched. At one bound I was again among civilized beings, renewing my resolution never again to travel alone as long as I remained in Africa.

The inmates of the coach were a French grisette and her lover, and an old Frenchwoman, who, to judge from her bulk, must have secured two places; for she alone occupied the centre seat. She was generous enough, however, to compress her enormous dimensions and make room for me. Upon hearing my story, and learning that I had not tasted food for twenty-four hours, compassion was aroused in the expansive bosom of my fair neighbor, and she drew forth a huge Bologna sausage, which, with tears in her eyes, she offered to me as a consolation for my sufferings. Noble and generous Dame Blanche! had I not been too weak at that moment, reduced as I was by hunger, fatigue, and anxiety, and had my arms been somewhat longer, I would have pressed her to my grateful heart in return for her kindness.

That evening I arrived at Tlemcen. I was scarcely installed in the hotel when I betook myself to my room and bed. I cannot say that I enjoyed a good night's rest, for I was somewhat feverish and nervous; and when in the morning I awoke and was called to breakfast, I found that I could not move, and every joint in my body felt as though it were dislocated.

Several Frenchmen who resided in the hotel called to see me; for Dame Blanche, who, in addition to her generous nature, was very talkative, and had a peculiar faculty of embellishing every thing she related, had not only noised abroad my adventure, but had added that I had been besieged by panthers and lions, and that at the moment the stage-coach came to my rescue I was engaged in a deadly combat with an ourang-outang five times my size. This narration naturally enough excited the curiosity and sympathy of all the inmates of the hotel; and it was probably on this account that I was treated with the greatest kindness, not only by the hotel-keeper, but by all the attendants. A charming little chambermaid who served me early in the morning with my *café au lait,* and who had expected to see me covered with wounds, possibly without a nose or ears, was astonished to find me all sound, and expressed her surprise by asking me if I was the person who had undergone the horrible adventures as related by Dame Blanche. A hearty embrace and a salute on her rosy cheek convinced her of one fact at least,—that my arms and face were all right and had not been injured by the ourang-outang.

I did not leave my room that day, but I sent to the French commander of the place a letter which had been given to me in Algiers by my friend Dr. H——; and that officer, having heard of my adventure, called on me and kindly offered me the freedom of his residence for any length of time I might feel inclined to remain in Tlemcen.

I must confess that at that moment I was tired of travelling. I thought I had had my share of African life, and expressed myself to that effect to the commander. He laughed heartily, saying that what I had experienced ought rather to be an inducement to continue, for it was only an initiation into real African life. "Well," said I, "if you call my adventures an initiation, I should like to know what the end must be, if not a *requiem in pacis.*"

The next morning I felt somewhat restored, but still was not my former self; and the doctor of the French garrison recommended me to take a Moorish bath, which he said would not only invigorate my bodily frame, but would have a beneficial and soothing effect on my agitated mind. I concluded to take the doctor's advice, and made my way at once to the best and cleanest bath-house in the city.

In the outer court of the establishment was a group of Arabs sitting cross-legged under an orange-grove, resting themselves after having taken their bath; while here and there, near the entrance of the inner court, stood other Arabs, clothed in the dress that Adam wore when he was driven from Paradise. These were the servants who waited on the visitors. Acquainting them with my desire, I was directed to a kind of office, where I had to deposit all my valuables; and then another official received my clothes, of which, with the aid of the attendants, I was soon stripped. This operation completed, I was covered with a piece of old camel-hair rug, and provided with a pair of sandals. In this not very picturesque costume I was led into a large hall, in which the temperature of the atmosphere was above 110° Fahr. In the centre of this hall was a high stone table, or rather a kind of stone altar, such as the Indians use for human sacrifices,—with this difference, that twelve men could have lain on it side by side. A little pad was placed where my head was to repose; and I was stretched on this altar, nothing being needed to complete the picture but the knife and the high-priest. In a few moments my body was covered with a violent perspiration, which continued for some time. In this state I was carried by two of the attendants to a warm-water fountain close by, and subjected to a hot-water shower-bath, applied with such force as to render it any thing but agreeable. This accomplished to the satisfaction of the attendants, I was subjected to the operation of squeezing, the officiating Arab kneading me with all his might, sometimes, indeed, so mercilessly that I feared for my ribs. He would catch me in a playful way, punch my chest, skate down my back with his bare feet, and perform all sorts of gymnastic feats, which to him were perhaps very amusing, but to me were exquisite torture. After having nearly exhausted himself with this pastime, he smacked his lips in token of satisfaction, and commenced to rub me with a handful of coarse cloths, still keeping up the liberal application of hot water. He then took some fine Kabyl soap, and made a lather, which he applied to my body, covering me literally an inch thick; and now for the first time since I had entered the so-called bath was I able to breathe with comfort. As soon as the lather showed signs of drying, buckets of hot water were thrown over me, drenching me from head to foot. After having been thus squeezed, pressed, kneaded, boxed, skated on, lathered, and doused, a turban was placed on my head, a sheet was wound around my unrefreshed body, and I was taken to the outer court to cool. Here was a row of mattresses, on one of which I was placed and covered with a piece of gauze, where I remained until I was perfectly dry. Then I received, as a finishing stroke, a new kneading, after which I was pronounced perfect. I was then led to the room where I had deposited my clothes, which I put on in haste, dreading lest some operation might have been forgotten. I felt somewhat relieved in mind, but was more exhausted in body than when I had entered this so-called delicious Moorish bath.

The same evening I was invited by a Frenchman with whom I had become acquainted to visit a Moorish house where the ceremony of circumcision was to be performed.

On such occasions, and especially when the father of the child is rich, the aristocracy of the place are generally present.

At eight o'clock we left our hotel and went direct to the house where the ceremony was to take place. It belonged to a rich Moor who was formerly a *cadi*, and who had over five hundred camels employed in the trade between Tlemcen and Morocco. His first-born son was now to be admitted into the Mohammedan faith.

When we arrived at the outer court, we found it filled with a crowd of the lower class of Moors and Arabs. In the centre was a large fountain, around which the musicians were stationed with their instruments,—cymbals like those of the wandering gipsies, drums of the most primitive fashion, iron triangles, flutes made from the branches of the willow-tree, and another instrument which I find it difficult to describe: it consisted of a large wooden frame, over which was drawn a dried raw cowhide; under this, at regular intervals, were suspended bells of various sizes, while at each side was a concave plate of copper, also furnished with bells. This instrument was played upon with two sticks, terminating in balls wrapped in cloth of goat's hair. Performed on alone, the sounds it produced were not altogether disagreeable; but when it was accompanied by the other instruments the discord was fearful.

Another of the instruments was a box, in the form of a coffin, the upper side of which was perforated with holes, and had wires stretched over it, somewhat like the strings of a violoncello. It was played with a bow formed of wires, and gave forth sounds which Europeans would hardly have termed musical.

At the first glance I thought it was really a coffin; for it was painted black, and, as if to confirm the impression conveyed by its shape, various inscriptions from the Koran were written on it in white paint.

When we entered the house, the dirty pack of Arabs and Moors were chanting in chorus verses from the Koran, accompanied by the musicians with their barbarous instruments. At the farther end of the court were congregated some fifty or sixty boys of various ages, whose chattering, combined with the discordant notes of the choristers and instrumental performers, was enough to drive a person of sensitive nerves to distraction.

We were invited to seat ourselves on some very rich carpets which were spread for the occasion; and after we had done so, coffee and pipes were brought to us by the servants of the house. Soon the invited guests began to arrive in considerable numbers, and took up their position on the carpet with us. The choristers having by this time exhausted the strength of their lungs, the demoniacal noise ceased,—a matter of self-congratulation to us,—and, in company with the musicians, they partook of coffee like the guests. I may be allowed to remark here that in Africa coffee is served up with the sediment, which renders the liquid very turbid and muddy-looking. The Algerine mode of preparing it differs greatly from the European. The bean is roasted of a dark-brown color, and is then broken in a wooden mortar into a coarse powder. The powder is put into a woollen bag shaped like a cone or a reversed sugar-loaf. This bag is then immersed in a large earthen jar full of boiling water, and is kept there for a quarter of an hour. The cups are half filled with boiled ground coffee from the woollen bag, and afterwards filled up with the liquid from the earthen jar. The coffee thus prepared is drunk without sugar by the Arabs; but Europeans are always served with sugar, whether at public houses or at private entertainments.

While we were leisurely sipping our coffee, some twenty or more Moorish ladies made their appearance, their faces covered with thick veils. They seated themselves opposite to us, in the same fashion as the men; and, as they were decidedly the most interesting portion of the assembly, they occupied the larger part of our attention.

Their attire cannot be better characterized than by calling it gorgeous. The reader has perhaps seen on the stage European actresses personating Moorish ladies; but he can never form an adequate idea of their grace and coquetry until he has seen a Moorish woman of the wealthy class. On this occasion I made a minute inspection of them, as far as a proper regard for their usages and customs would permit me. One of those present engaged my attention in a special degree. She was about fourteen years of age, and had been married the day before. I have seen full-grown women with remarkably small feet, in Mexico, in the Spanish province of Andalusia, and among the Indians of Tehuantepec; but the feet of this young Moorish bride were the most diminutive I ever beheld. They seemed like those of a child not over seven years of age, rather than a woman's. They were encased in rich gold-embroidered coverings of exquisite workmanship, which in themselves would have fixed the attention and called forth the admiration of the beholder. Around her beautifully-modelled ankles were rings of gold ornamented with turquoises, and the band that fastened her trousers, which were of satin of a yellowish tint, was secured by a golden clasp, from which hung two silver tassels that gracefully fell over her feet. From her waist hung, in deep plaits, reaching to her knees, a dark-brown skirt of a rich Turkish fabric, around the border of which was a garland of oak-leaves embroidered with silver, and intermingled with little balls of pure gold, forming miniature clusters of grapes. Above this skirt was another, of a green color, adorned with gold fringe, but so short as to display the embroidery of the under dress; while around her slender waist was fastened a scarf of the finest camel's hair. These scarfs, I was informed, are sometimes sold at the enormous price of from fifteen hundred to two thousand *duros* (dollars) apiece. The one in question was very tastefully arranged, one end of it falling in front and the other behind. The bow that secured it in front was adorned with a clasp thickly set with diamonds and pearls; and to the end that hung down were attached several large-sized pearls, which at a distance looked like little bells, and which the lady knew how to display to the best advantage. The corsage, which was very short, consisted of white satin, without any trimming other than a scarcely perceptible gold fringe or hem on the upper part. Over this she wore

17

a tightly-fitting Zouave jacket of red damask, without sleeves, the border of which was adorned with gold embroidery representing very small leaves. Her neck and arms, of a contour that a sculptor might have despaired to imitate, were entirely bare, except that a pearl necklace of two rows adorned the one, and bracelets of the costliest French workmanship graced the other. Her turban, studded with precious stones, was very small, and was coquettishly set on one side of her head; but from the top and centre hung the invidious veil, hiding from view the face whose beauty I could only imagine. I can assure my reader that the inventor of the stupid custom of veil-wearing did not receive many benedictions from me on that day.

The rest of the fair guests were attired with similar profusion of material and color; but I was so completely taken up with the appearance of the young bride that I had no time to note any details of the dresses of the others.

After the customary salaams had been exchanged, my attention was drawn to the little urchins, who made a sudden rush towards the principal entrance, stumbling over one another in their haste to reach the spot, many of them being thrown down by their stronger companions. As if to add to the general confusion, the choristers and musicians again began to indulge in their frantic shouts and hideous noise, and it seemed to us, ignorant as we were of the routine of the ceremony, that something extraordinary was about to take place. Mingling with the crowd, we saw a man with a long white beard, dressed in a white burnouse, and accompanied by two other Arabs, who were scattering almonds and raisins among the little folks from two large baskets which they carried in their hands. It is, it seems, a command of the Koran, and therefore an essential part of the ceremony, that the small fry be permitted to enjoy themselves to the full on an occasion like this. The tumbling and scrambling, screaming and yelling, of the young folks, in their energetic endeavors to get a full share of the sweetmeats, amused me exceedingly.

When order had been re-established in some slight degree, and the passage cleared, the man with the white beard approached the house; whereupon the whole company, men as well as women, drew near to kiss his hand. This was the marabout who was to perform the ceremony.

As I have remarked in the earlier part of my narrative, the marabouts are looked upon as saints, and they are held in the deepest reverence by all Mohammedans.

The one who was to officiate upon this occasion seated himself (after he had been respectfully greeted by the whole assemblage) in a corner of the spacious court, where a divan had been laid expressly for his use. Immediately thereupon, the mother of the child in whose honor all present had congregated, approached, leading by the hand her first-born, a boy apparently nine or ten years of age, who was dressed in white silk trousers and a red velvet jacket adorned with gold lace. He was conducted directly to the marabout, who, rising, stretched out his hands, and, in a low, measured voice, repeated a prayer, at the same time invoking a blessing on the child who was about to become a member of the Mohammedan faith. During the chanting of the prayer, the audience, with the exception of my friend and myself,—the only persons in the room who were not be-

lievers in Islam,—prostrated themselves on their faces.
The prayer and blessing finished, the marabout em-
braced the child, and lifted him up three times, after
which he led him to all the ladies present, each of
whom, raising her veil with great precaution lest her
face should be seen by the men, imprinted a kiss on his
rosy lips. My friend remarked to me that as far as
this part of the ceremony was concerned, he would not
object to becoming himself a follower of the Prophet.

When the boy had made this agreeable round, he was
lifted up once more by the marabout and taken into another court, from which a broad staircase led to the upper
apartments. The ladies were invited into another room,
where refreshments had been prepared for them; while
I and my friend were asked to follow the marabout and
witness the ceremony. We forthwith proceeded up-
stairs, and were ushered into a spacious room, furnished
in the resplendent style which seems to be the rule
among the wealthy Moors of Algeria. Rich cushions
heavily embroidered with gold extended along the
walls, and in the centre was a large bed, with thick
damask hangings. In front of this stood four of the
nearest relations of the Moor, each holding a large,
old-fashioned silver candlestick with a lighted wax
taper in it. The father had in his hand a red velvet
cushion, on which lay the open Koran; while one of
the attendants of the marabout held a silver salver, on
which were a richly-chased goblet of the same metal
and a bottle containing some sort of liquor.

The child was on his knees, with his face bowed to the
ground, and the marabout was standing over him with
arms outstretched as if in earnest prayer. When all who
had been invited to witness the ceremony were seated,

and perfect silence reigned in the room, the marabout lifted the child from the floor and took him behind the bed-curtains, followed by the attendants, the father, and the bearers of the candlesticks. A little bell was then sounded, which seemed to be a signal to the choristers and instrumental performers in the outer court to renew their frightful discord; for they instantly set to work with hearty good will, producing at least twice their former clamor,—with the view, I suppose, of drowning the cries of the little sufferer who was sealing by his blood his confirmation in the Mohammedan faith. After the lapse of about fifteen minutes, the marabout reappeared, but the little fellow remained behind.

We were now invited to partake of some refreshments, and of course accepted the invitation; but I very much regretted not having been permitted to witness the whole of the ceremony, as my scientific curiosity had been excited to the utmost.

The aspect of Tlemcen is very pleasing, especially from the north. The surrounding plain is covered with olive-trees, giving it the appearance of a forest. The fruit of these olives belongs to the natives, who in this place appear to be further advanced in civilization and to enjoy greater prosperity than any I had met with elsewhere.

While Abd-el-Kader resided at Tlemcen, the natives were wretchedly poor, owing to the breaking up of all business by the constant wars which the great chief waged against the French. This place was the head-quarters of the Emir; and it was a post of great importance to him in a military view, since it afforded a convenient and undisturbed means of communication with Morocco, whence he received much of his war material. Supplies also came to him by way of the Tafna, of which the Isser is one of the tributaries. These last came direct from Gibraltar; and it was whispered at the time that the English had something to do with furnishing them.

In 1842 Tlemcen was occuped by the French troops under General Bedeau, who made himself noted among the large number of French generals to whom at various times the government of Algeria has been intrusted.

Immediately after his appointment, he set about weakening the power of Abd-el-Kader in the valley of the Upper Tafna. This he did by appealing to the republican instincts of the Kabyl population, who were averse to submission to a central power. He carefully fostered the jealousy which already existed in regard to the Emir, and entered into a league with all who were discontented with the old order of things. The inhabitants of Nedrouma, a town which lies to the west of the Lower Tafna, were the first to join this alliance with the foreigner; and the defection spread so rapidly that the Emir was finally obliged to abandon Tlemcen and retreat to the south, after which the whole country, from Tlemcen to the Mediterranean, fell into the hands of the conqueror, who has retained it ever since.

Tlemcen is not more than ten miles from the frontier of Morocco; and, although the Arabs in that part of the French dominion are kept in subjugation, those who live on the Morocco side of the frontier-line are the deadliest foes of the French, and never let slip an opportunity of striking a blow at the invader. They are constantly crossing the frontier and committing the most terrible acts of brigandage.

As there are no treaty relations between Algeria and Morocco, criminals from either country flee for refuge to the other. Hence it is that so many outrages are committed here, as the perpetrator finds no difficulty in escaping after he has worked out his purpose.

During my stay at Tlemcen I witnessed a number of executions; for when a Morocco brigand is caught he is shot by the French with very slight ceremony, because their robberies are generally accompanied with murder, and it is considered the best policy to hang the criminal as soon as caught. The country is infested with these brigands, and it is very unsafe to venture far from the city without adequate protection. The farmers around the city have instituted night patrols; but during dark and stormy nights these are of very little service. For this reason a strong force of spahis is constantly on the watch. They keep up a kind of espionage, and when they get a clue to an intended attack they unite to prevent it, or, if too late for that, to arrest the perpetrators of the outrage. When a criminal is caught, a *procès-verbal* is drawn up, and one hour afterwards a dose of five lead pills is administered to the unwilling patient, curing him at once of all the ills of life.

In the year 1830, Tlemcen was little better than a mass of ruins, the result of the war. In the highest part of the city is still to be seen a strong walled fortress, similar to the Kasbah at Algiers. This, in former times, was the palace of the chief, and was known by the name of *Mechouar*.

This palace, or fortress, has its history. Several years before the French conquest, the Arabs in this section of the country resolved to throw off the Turkish yoke, and commenced active hostilities without a moment's warning. The garrison of Tlemcen, being too far away from head-quarters to hope for reinforcements before they should be overpowered, took refuge in the Mechouar, and for nearly five years successfully resisted the attacks of the Arabs. What makes this circumstance all the more remarkable is that the garrison consisted of but two hundred men, Turks and Koloughs, while the Arabs numbered at least two thousand.

Many are the stories told in Tlemcen of the renowned chief Abd-el-Kader, who so long held sway over the city and the surrounding country; and, as I have ever been deeply interested in the history of great men, I obtained here many interesting data concerning this modern Jugurtha.

The Arabs now under French rule speak with a feeling of pride of their celebrated chief being of the same age as the present Emperor Napoleon. Both were born in the year 1808, and on the same day; but the Emir cannot boast of princely blood. He was the son of Mahiddin, a marabout of the Hachem tribe, in the neighborhood of Mascara, and belonged to a clan whose ancestors were celebrated no less for their scholarship than for their sanctity; for his forefathers had for several generations presided over a college, called the Guetna of Sidi Mahiddin, founded by one of his remote progenitors.

Abd-el-Kader received the best education that this college could afford, under the immediate supervision of his father; and the pains taken with him in youth, combined with assiduous application to study, helped to make him, in after-life, the remarkable man he proved to be. The extraordinary ascendency which he obtained over his people in later years, however, was chiefly the result of an occurrence said to have taken place in his boyish life. The story was related to me by a native, and is in substance as follows:—

When, in the year 1832, the Arabs saw their country falling piecemeal into the hands of the French, they offered the supreme power to Mahiddin, the father of Abd-el-Kader, promising implicit obedience to him as their chief, and urging him to lead them against the common enemy. The old man, however, declined the arduous honor, at the same time advising them to elect, instead, his son. By way of sustaining his opinion as to the fitness of the latter, he related the following incident. Some years before, when on a pilgrimage to the holy place of Mecca, accompanied by his eldest son, he had met a *fakir*, who offered him three apples. "One I give to thee," said the holy man, "one to the boy who is now with thee, and the third is for thy youngest son, whom thou hast left at home, and who at no very distant day will rise to the dignity of Sultan."

Meaningless as this incident may appear, and uncertain though it be whether it ever really transpired or was but an invention of the old marabout, it told forcibly on the superstitious minds of the Arabs. His youngest son was proclaimed chief of the tribes that were thronging to the defence of their country against the invader, and was at once installed as Emir of Mascara. In this office his abilities soon made themselves manifest. He it was who, by the example of his dauntless courage, taught his people to disregard the fire of artillery, of which till that time they had had a dread that seemed to be invincible.

One year after his elevation to the post of Emir of

Mascara, he took possession of Tlemcen; and thenceforward his power rapidly increased, so that it was not long until his supremacy was acknowledged by all the tribes between the confines of Morocco and the river Chelif. In 1835 he crossed the Chelif, took Cherchell and Tenez, pushed on to Milianah, from thence to Medeah, and soon became master of the entire province of Titterie.

Here, on the 29th of June, he encountered the French, numbering twenty-five hundred men, under General Trézel. In the engagement that ensued, the Emir was victorious, entirely routing the enemy and capturing one howitzer,—the first he ever possessed. This defeat of the French was the severest they ever experienced on Algerine soil; and, to avenge it, Marshal Clausel, accompanied by the Duke of Orleans, led an imposing expedition against Mascara in the following November, consisting of eleven thousand men. Reaching Mascara on the 5th of December, they found it abandoned, Abd-el-Kader, with all his followers, having withdrawn. The French troops, disappointed of their prey, applied the torch to the deserted city, and soon reduced it to ashes.

From that time forward the career of Abd-el-Kader became a part of French history; and those who are familiar with the story of the French conquest of Algeria cannot refrain from admiring the hero who battled unremittingly for his country's independence until, overpowered by a formidable disciplined army, he fell a prisoner into the hands of his enemy. Had he possessed but a dozen cannon in 1834, the probabilities are that he would have been to-day sole master of Barbary.

His name is revered by the Arabs; and many an hour have I listened with the deepest interest to their accounts of his deeds of valor, the details of which will doubtless be transmitted by his admiring countrymen from father to son for generations to come.

Tlemcen consists of an old and a new town. The former was almost entirely destroyed during the siege of the Mechouar, which now serves as a barrack, hospital, and storehouse for the garrison. From the ramparts of this fortress I obtained a delightful view of the valley of the Tafna, the scenery of which is not surpassed in beauty by any other locality I ever visited in my rambles about the world.

The new town—that is to say, the lower part of Tlemcen—is small, consisting of but five streets, and is inhabited chiefly by tradesmen and Jews, who make a living by traffic with the garrison.

The natives trade mostly with those who come from Morocco, who are easily known by the villainous expression of their faces and their peculiar style of dress. They do not wear the burnouse, but instead a brown-colored tunic with black stripes running lengthwise, similar to the dress worn by the Beni-Mozabites, one of the tribes of the Sahara.

About one mile from Tlemcen is a celebrated ruin, which the French commander invited me to visit. I cordially acceded to his proposition, making it a condition, however, that we were to explore no subterranean passages; for the adventure at Bona was too fresh in my memory to allow me to gratify my curiosity in any further under-ground researches.

The ruin in question is evidently the remains of an ancient fortification; and it dates farther back than the

old town. Five circles of works are distinctly trace-
able; and the distance from each wall to the next is so
great that I was twelve minutes in traversing it. These
intervening spaces are now covered with a growth of
huge olive-trees, the oldest I ever met with in my
travels. I was assured by persons conversant with the
ages of trees that these olives must be at least seven
hundred or eight hundred years old. They were doubtless planted after the completion of the fortifications;
and this circumstance led me to make some inquiries
concerning the antiquity of the latter.

Tlemcen, in days gone by, was a flourishing city.
Its population numbered over two hundred thousand,
and its wealth was enormous. During its age of gran-
deur a sultan of Mostaganem besieged it, and, unable to
reduce it, he established a permanent military camp
outside of its gates, which soon became the nucleus of a
new city. His army was composed of recruits from all
parts of Barbary, and was so numerous that his cavalry
alone brought from the mouth of the Tafna, in the
folds of their burnouses, the material for building the
wall around the camp. From the earth thus brought
hither by the cavalry was also made a cement of which
the secret of the manufacture is now lost.

The new city grew as if by magic, and in its centre
rose a mosque of surpassing beauty, one-half built by
Jews and the other half by Mohammedans. The Mohammedan part of the structure is yet standing; the
other is entirely in ruins.

After a siege of years, Tlemcen fell before the power
of the sultan. Soon afterwards the mushroom city that
had grown up at its gates was entirely destroyed; and
nothing is now to be seen of it but time-worn ruins.

Our guide pointed out to us the Mansouhra, or palace of the former sovereigns. All that is left of this is a wall that formed either part of the palace itself or of a defence surrounding it. It is six feet thick, and twenty-five feet high. There are indications of the existence, originally, of square towers on this wall, at intervals of from forty to fifty yards. The circumference of the whole is a little more than a mile. Within the area which it encloses is a remarkable piece of antique architecture,—the ruins of a mosque the minaret of which is rent from top to bottom. This minaret is still standing, although it is nearly one hundred feet high and in all probability was built at least nine hundred years ago. Like the Mansouhra, it has every appearance of having been surrounded originally by a wall; for in its well-preserved ruins holes are visible, which were doubtless intended for the convenience of the bowmen and spearmen in repelling the attacks of an enemy.

I brought away with me some of the material of which this wall was composed. It is not a natural stone, but a kind of concrete, moulded into blocks, which are cemented with the same substance. It is so hard that it is very difficult to break it. I sent a small piece of it to the Imperial Museum of Vienna; and another I kept for more than a year, but lost it, with many other curiosities, when I was shipwrecked on the coast of Florida.

I examined the interior of the minaret, and found it to contain eight stories. The exterior is elaborately ornamented in the most finished Arabian style. In the lower part of the structure are several carved stones, probably brought hither from the ruins of some Roman city after its destruction by the Vandals.

18

These ruins, for their magnitude and architecture, are without exception the most interesting to be met with in the northern part of Africa. Their elaboration casts doubt on the authenticity of the story that they are the remains of a permanent camp built for the purpose of reducing Tlemcen; for the construction of the buildings and fortifications could not have occupied less than a quarter of a century, while the necessary expenditure must have largely outbalanced the amount of the booty to be expected from the beleaguered city.

I have since made diligent search in the most celebrated libraries of Europe for some reliable history of Tlemcen, but have been able to find very little light thrown on the subject of its antiquity. There can be no doubt, however, that the city has passed through many and great vicissitudes.

The forest of olive-trees which surrounds the ruins has paths cut through it, for the convenience of promenaders. The ancient name has been dropped, as is the case wherever the conquering invader has set his foot; and the wood is now called by the French "Le Bois de Boulogne."

The day after I visited these ruins, I went to the village of Sidi-Bou-Medine, in company with a young Moor whose acquaintance I had formed at Oran. He spoke the French language admirably, having lived in Paris for two years. This village is deemed so sacred that Christians are not permitted to reside in it. Thanks, however, to the influence of my companion, I was allowed to enter the mosque and its sanctuary, with no restriction other than that of leaving my boots at the threshold,—a rule to which faithful and faithless alike must bow.

The mosque of the marabout is a perfect *bijou*. It contains the tomb of Sidi-Bou-Medine and Sidi-Absalom, who are buried together. The sarcophagus is draped with rich carpet; and on the walls hang innumerable offerings of the faithful. In front of the tomb is a screen covered with banners, trophies of warfare or presents to the saints. Beside the tomb of the marabouts are buried the remains of five persons whose devotion during their lives to the memory of the holy men had entitled them to the distinction of interment in these sacred precincts.

Connected with the mosque is an apartment for the accommodation of pilgrims who visit the shrine and pass the night there.

In the outer court is a small well, the water of which is in high repute among the pilgrims for its miraculous virtues, but which to my taste could lay claim to no more remarkable quality than that of a slight flavor of iron.

Adjoining the mosque is a school for the children of the village. Here I saw little ones not more than four years old, with pieces of parchment in their hands, from which they were studying the Arabic alphabet.

In Tlemcen I made the acquaintance of a renegade German whose family name was Schneider, but who now rejoiced in the Arabic appellation of Ibrahim. He had been brought up to the trade of a gunsmith, had come to Algeria in early life, and during Abd-el-Kader's supremacy had been made director of the arsenal at Tlemcen. As a reward for his constant adherence to the fortunes of the Emir and the zeal he displayed in the cause of Algerine independence, he was finally appointed *Zapatapa*, or keeper of the great

seal of state,—a position similar to that occupied by
the Neapolitan slave Mariano Stinca under Hammu-
dan Pasha.

Ibrahim accompanied Abd-el-Kader in all his campaigns; but when the Emir surrendered to the French
he would not permit his devoted follower to share his
captivity. The latter thereupon retired to private life,
settling in the vicinity of Tlemcen. It was rumored
that the Emir had intrusted him with the secret of the
hiding-place of his treasures; and many believed that
thence Ibrahim obtained the wealth which enabled him
to live in such luxurious style.

He was always overjoyed to meet any one who could
speak his native tongue; and when I was introduced to
him he did not attempt to disguise his pleasure. In fact,
the warmth and heartiness of his greeting made me
feel almost at once as if I had found in this out-of-the-
way part of the world an intimate friend from whom I
had been parted for many years; and I very thankfully
accepted his pressing invitation to make his country-
seat my home until the spirit of adventure should im-
pel me to leave Tlemcen.

Had this man been educated in a European university instead of in a blacksmith's shop, before his
appointment to the office of *Zapatapa* to the Emir, the
French would, in my opinion, have found the conquest
of Algeria a much more difficult problem than it proved
to be. His house was built and furnished almost entirely on European models; and he still showed himself true to the memory of Vaterland by having sour-
crout served on his table at least once a week.

His memory was an inexhaustible storehouse of
anecdotes and reminiscences of his campaigns with the

Emir; and he never wearied of talking of the stirring events in which he had taken part. His life was one uninterrupted chain of thrilling incidents of the most varied character; and I used to sit in rapt silence listening to him by the hour. Often since have I regretted that I did not take notes of his narratives; for had I done so I might now fill volume after volume with the account of the heroic struggle of the Algerines, making use of colors very different from those into which French authors dip their pencils for the gratification of the national vanity of themselves and their readers.

Once in the course of our conversation I suggested to him to write a history of his campaigns. He replied that, although nothing could give him greater pleasure than the opportunity of relating the incidents connected with his life in Africa, he had not the slightest ambition, in his old age, to become an auto-biographer. He looked back with satisfaction on his early career, and now enjoyed the peaceful life which his energy had won, but cared nothing whatever for the plaudits of the world.

In public, Ibrahim always wore the Moorish costume; but in the privacy of home he assumed his early European customs and dress,—with the exception, as to the latter, of the fez cap, which never left his head, principally, I suppose, on account of his being entirely bald. One room in his house was fitted up in the Moorish style, for the reception of visitors of his adopted creed; but even here the marks of European taste were displayed. The divans looked rather like lounges, and the seat he occupied when the room was in use stood in the centre of the wall that faced the one entrance-

door, and resembled those used by the Presidents of
the Spanish-American republics. Behind this seat,
and suspended on the wall, was a piece of red velvet
embroidered with gold, around which were tastefully
arranged various implements of warfare,—spears, yata-
ghans, scimitars, and long-barrelled muskets and rifles,
—all richly inlaid with gold and silver, and several of
them studded with diamonds and other precious stones.
Above this was a tablet of black marble, on which
were inscribed two maxims from the Koran, which may
be translated as follows :—" If the word be worth silver,
then silence is worth gold," and, "Wealth does not belong to the miser, but the miser to wealth."

My friend and host, when a humorous mood seized
him, would sometimes relate many amusing incidents
in connection with the amorous adventures he had been
concerned in shortly after his arrival in Africa.

The Mohammedan beauties, he told me, are very
prone to intrigue with the Christians ; but it is attended
with great difficulty and danger. An interview can be
obtained only on the terraces or flat roofs of the houses,
where the women usually appear without their veils.
My friend had once had an opportunity, while yet a
Christian, of courting a beautiful woman belonging to
a Moor ; and on one occasion he asked her what the
consequence would be if their meetings were discovered.
She replied, " Oh, the consequence would not amount
to much for you : you would merely lose your head.
But they would carry me on an ass around the city,
with my face unveiled and exposed to the view of the
populace, and, as a final punishment, they would throw
me into the sea."

This information had a tendency to check any desire

on my part to make the acquaintance of the Moorish
ladies, and even gave me an uneasy sense of danger
when in close proximity to one of them.

Intrigues of this kind with the Jewish beauties are
attended with no such risks. The best place to make
their acquaintance is the Jewish cemetery, where they
assemble in great numbers every first day of the new
moon, each provided with a pitcher containing lime dis-
solved in water, with which they whitewash the tomb-
stones of their deceased relatives,—an operation which
they believe is peculiarly grateful to the spirits of the
departed.

In these cemeteries the graves are not marked by
mounds: they are level with the general surface, and
over each grave is placed a flagstone: in this stone is
inserted a small square medallion in marble, on which
are inscribed, in Hebrew characters, the name of the
deceased, and the dates of birth and death. The graves
are placed as close together as possible; and the stones
give to the cemetery, at a distance, the appearance of a
tiled parquet.

My host was married to a beautiful Jewess, his third
wife. She was from Tripoli, and was a descendant of
one of those families who, by the unwise policy of the
government of Spain, had been driven from their native
country and forced to take refuge among the people of
Barbary. Whether on account of the extraordinary
beauty of his wife, or from the indulgent spirit that
sometimes characterizes old age, I know not, but he
seemed to me to be governed by her most trivial desire:
in other words, he was henpecked. I was reminded by
their little domestic passages of the spirited sarcastic
verses composed by the brother-in-law of the Dutch

consul of Tunis on the occasion of the Jews being forbidden by the then reigning Bey to wear any other
head-covering than the three-cornered hat. These verses
are familiar to the Jews of Algiers even to this day;
and, as it is hardly likely that the reader has ever seen
them, I take the liberty of placing them before him.

THE THREE-CORNERED HAT.

(*Le Chapeau à Cornes.*)

CHORUS OF ISRAELITES.

Malheureux Juifs, versez de larmes!
C'en est fait de vos chapeaux ronds.
O jour de deuil! O jour d'alarmes!
Témoin du plus grand des affronts!

THE POLICEMAN.

Peuple Juif, couvrez votre tête
De ce chapeau, de ce bonnet;
Du pouvoir je suis l'interprète,
Soyez soumis au grand décret.

THE JEWISH RABBI.

Quand sur le Sinaï la puissance sans bornes
A Moïse donna des loix pour ses enfans,
Moïse descendît du mont avec *deux cornes:*
N'êtes-vous pas ses descendans?

COMPLAINT OF THE YOUNG JEW TO HIS BELOVED.

Pleurez, descendantes jolies
D'Esther, de Ruth et de Sara;
Gémissez, nos douces amies,
Du grand coup qui nous accabla.
Hélas! nos malheurs sont sans bornes;
On nous oblige, malgré nous,
De porter de *chapeaux à cornes*
Avant que d'être vos époux.

ANSWER OF THE YOUNG JEWESS TO HER LOVER.

Ah ! vos amantes désolées
Ne cessent de vous répéter :
« Vos têtes bien ou mal coiffées
« Ne vous empechent pas d'aimer.
« Le tendre amour n'a point de bornes,
« Du sort il sait braver les coups ;
« Et craint-on des *chapeaux à cornes*
« Lorsqu'on désire d'être époux ? »

COMPLAINT OF THE MARRIED JEW TO HIS WIFE.

Pleurez sur nos peines cruelles,
Femmes, le malheur nous poursuit :
Désormais vos époux fidèles
Ne seront qu'en bonnet de nuit ;
Car leur honte serait sans bornes,
Si l'on disait, parlant de nous :
« A leur tour de *chapeaux à cornes*
« Ornent le front de ces époux ! . . . »

ANSWER OF THE JEWESS TO HER HUSBAND.

Fils de Jacob, pourquoi ces plaintes ?
Pourquoi ces pleurs et ces regrets ?
Fils de Jacob, calmez vos craintes,
Jetez loin de vous ces bonnets.
La douleur doit avoir des bornes ;
Sauvez vos frères d'embarras ;
Reprenez les *chapeaux à cornes :*
Tant de Chrétiens n'en ont-ils pas ?

During my stay in Tlemcen I witnessed for the first time the punishment by bastinado. It was in one of the Moorish courts, where a young Arab, accused and convicted of theft, was sentenced to receive one hundred strokes on the soles of his feet. A European could not survive the infliction of a punishment like this; but the Arab, although he made a great outcry and called lustily for the aid of the Prophet while the blows were being administered, ran away immediately afterwards as nimbly as if nothing had happened. This may be accounted for by the fact that the natives of the lower class generally go barefoot, and the soles of their feet become so callous that they are in a great measure insensible to blows.

The Moorish criminal code provides only three kinds of punishment. An assassin is condemned to death, without appeal. The trial is held in public, and as soon as the accused is proved guilty the sentence is pronounced and carried into effect. The only avenue of escape for the criminal is the willingness of the murdered person's relatives to accept a sum of money in satisfaction for the life of their kinsman. In cases of robbery, the culprit's hand is chopped off; and in order to effect a rapid cure the stump is immediately dipped into boiling pitch, which prevents mortification, and, forming a crust over the wound, heals it without the aid of a physician,—and probably much more effectually ; for Moorish doctors are not remarkable for scientific attainments. For trifling offences the punishment is the bastinado or a fine.

Very curious decisions are frequently given in civil cases. My host, who accompanied me in my sight-seeing through the city, related to me one in particular which amused me exceedingly.

An Arab had a quantity of hen's eggs, and his neighbor was the owner of a hen. The two agreed that a suitable number of eggs be placed under the hen, and to divide the chickens equally between them, when hatched. It happened that but thirteen live birds came forth ; whereupon a dispute arose as to the proprietorship of the odd chicken. Not being able to settle it between themselves, they brought the brood with the mother-bird to court, and appealed to the cadi. That worthy, after duly pondering the question, ordered chickens and hen to be handed over to his cook, and sentenced each of the litigants to receive twenty-five blows of the bastinado, concluding his sentence with the sage remark that the example he made of these two unfortunates would tend to prevent neighbors from disputing about trifling matters.

Laughable as a decision of this kind undoubtedly is, we would not have to go very far out of the United States to find it paralleled. During my residence of several years in Mexico, I witnessed many an instance, in the courts, of injustice quite as flagrant as that of the cadi. The Moor, in fact, has the advantage of the Mexican; for the case of the former is settled at once, while the unlucky Mexican is harassed and baffled by the law's delay until the object for which he is striving has been swallowed up by judges and lawyers, and the only consolation he has, if he wins his case, is the rather doubtful one of paying the costs.

The time that I had fixed for my sojourn in Tlemcen was rapidly drawing to a close, and, believing that I had seen all in the city that was worth the seeing, I had now only to choose between accompanying the French expedition to the Sahara, and returning to Algiers, there to await an opportunity of taking passage either direct to America or to one of the Spanish possessions in the Atlantic, whence I could readily make my way to the United States.

My worthy host and his beautiful wife insisted warmly that I should prolong my stay; but, as there

was nothing more to engage my attention, I told them
I had resolved to decide within twelve hours whether I
should turn my steps in the direction of the Desert or
that of the land of freedom. Seeing that it was useless
to endeavor to persuade me further, they ceased from
their solicitations; and in the evening Ibrahim told
me, with an air of exceeding mystery, that, as I was inflexible in my determination to leave them, he intended
to give me a feast, so that if I ever returned to Europe
I should be able to tell more of Eastern life than the
ordinary class of travellers. His words and manner excited my curiosity, not being able to surmise what was
the nature of the surprise in store for me; but all I
could elicit from him was the good-humored evasion,
" Wait till to-morrow."

The following morning, as I was walking in the
garden attached to the house, thinking that the whole
family was still fast asleep, I suddenly came upon
Madame Ibrahim, sipping her coffee in a bower of
jasmines, which in that country attain a remarkable
height. She at once invited me to be seated and join
her in a cup of the beverage. Rather on account of
the opportunity of conversing with her than from any
desire to break my fast, I accepted her invitation. As
I have already said, Madame Ibrahim was a beautiful
woman; and now, as I saw her in her *demi-négligé*,
a white cashmere gown thrown carelessly around her
form, the loose and wide sleeves giving a glimpse of an
arm of dazzling whiteness, her tiny bare feet only partially covered by slippers, I could hardly refrain from
envying my aged host the possession of such a treasure.

During our conversation, I made several allusions to

the surprise her husband had in store for me; but on that subject she maintained an impenetrable reserve, and I soon found that I could do nothing better than patiently await the appointed hour, which was ten o'clock.

The flight of time was accelerated by the presence of my beautiful hostess; and it seemed but a few minutes ere the dial indicated the hour of ten,—at which moment, with all the punctuality of an Englishman, Ibrahim came in search of me.

In front of the house were three spirited horses, for the use of my host, his wife, and myself; and, having arranged our toilet, we mounted and set out, Ibrahim leading the way, towards the northern side of the city.

After a ride of about forty minutes, across a plain covered with date-trees and groves of orange and lime trees, we came to a spot where stood a romantic-looking edifice, which forcibly reminded me of the charming villas that abound in the environs of Florence. On an elevation of some two hundred feet rose a miniature palace, embowered in densest foliage. Its architecture was a tasteful combination of the Moorish, Italian, and Ionic orders. The grounds were surrounded by a thick-set hedge of cactus,—the *Agave Africana*,—and were laid out in the style of the pleasure-gardens of the European nobility.

The entrance to the grounds was through an artistically constructed rustic gate; and from this several winding paths led to the principal façade of the mansion. Not more than twenty yards off, and encircling the house without any sign of having been directed by human hands, ran a little brook, whose waters here and there fell in miniature cascades over the rocks and filled the air with their pleasing murmur.

Four or five rustic bridges were thrown over the brook, so as to give access to the mansion, which stood on the uppermost of three symmetrically arranged terraces. These terraces were encircled by grape-vines; and as, at the time of my visit, the vines were in full bearing, the general effect was that of a vast garland.

I very naturally inquired who was the proprietor of this miniature Eden; but my host persistently declined to satisfy my curiosity. When we arrived at the main entrance, four negroes, dressed tastefully in the style so frequently to be observed in Constantinople, made their appearance, and, humbly saluting us in the Moorish fashion, assisted us to alight, and led away our horses.

We now ascended six broad white marble steps, and entered an extensive corridor, Ibrahim preceding, his wife and myself following in silence. The corridor ex-tended along the four sides of the mansion, which mea-sured about one hundred yards on each side. At inter-vals of six yards rose tastefully-carved columns, sup-porting the ceiling, which also formed part of the roof. Each of these columns was encircled with climbing vines, loaded with brilliant-colored flowers; while from column to column hung festoons of the beautiful and fragrant wax-flower.

In the interior wall of the corridor, opposite the central points between the columns, were niches, in which were placed masterpieces of Italian sculpture; while on the floor between the niches stood bronze vases, some of which contained huge glass globes filled with goldfish, and in others grew rare plants nurtured into exuberant growth by the intelligent care of a European gardener. The floor was paved with tiles of black and white marble; and here and there stood small tables inlaid with mosaics of exquisite workmanship, while beside each table was a chair of fine wicker-work. From the ceiling hung a variety of gilded and highly-ornamented cages, containing a vast number of singing-birds of beautiful plumage, that made the air vocal with their sweet notes.

At the centre and corners of each side of the corridor hung a heavy gilt chandelier, bearing from forty to fifty large wax candles, and giving to the whole an air of princely luxury.

Amazed at the profusion of beautiful objects, I could not help stopping to cast an admiring glance around me. The garden especially attracted my attention. Here and there, rising above the thick foliage, could be seen bowers of various forms,—the Chinese pagoda, the Turkish kiosk, the English summer-house, each furnished in accordance with its architecture; while at the farther end a large space surrounded by a high iron railing was set apart for a magnificent specimen of the African lion, and near this was a majestic ostrich, sunning itself in its spacious prison.

In the centre of the garden was a miniature lake, in which floated gracefully a number of black and white swans, pursuing the gold-fish that now and then rose to the surface as if to inhale the delicious aroma distilled from the flowers that had been brought from every clime to adorn this princely estate.

If all these surroundings gave cause for astonishment, much more did the interior arrangements of the mansion. Following my host, I was led into a vesti-

bule which might perhaps be more correctly styled the
reception-room. The stuccoed ceiling rose in the form
of a cupola, the centre of which was composed of stained
glass, resplendent in the rays of the morning sun. The
floor was covered with a heavy Turkish carpet; and
instead of the Eastern furniture which I naturally
looked for, I beheld sofas, arm-chairs, lounges, tête-
à-têtes, tables, every thing of the latest European
fashion, even to an exceedingly fine piano. With the
exception of the ceiling, the apartment was, in fact, just
such a reception-room as one might expect to see in
a mansion of the Faubourg St. Germain in Paris.

I could no longer repress my curiosity; and I begged
my fair companion to inform me where we were. She,
however, simply pointed to her lord and master, who
at that moment seated himself, motioning me to a chair
directly opposite to him.

He touched a silver bell lying on one of the tables,
whereupon a handsome Moorish girl, attired in the
fantastic but charming style of the East, made her appearance, bearing a salver on which were placed a bottle
of champagne and several Bohemian wine-glasses of
exquisite workmanship. Placing these in front of
Ibrahim, she disappeared as noiselessly and rapidly as
she had entered the room.

After we had sat in silence for a few moments, which
were occupied by me in staring with astonishment at
all around me, my host informed me that at last he was
about to gratify my curiosity concerning the inmates
of this palace.

"You are," said he, "in the house of my former
master, Abd-el-Kader,—a house of which I am proud
to say I was the architect, and which was built for the

reception of two beautiful women, of whom one was a princess and the other a slave." Here my friend came to a pause; and although my curiosity was now more excited than ever, I asked no questions; for experience had taught me that, with Ibrahim, the more one asked the less one learned, and that the best way was to let him follow uninterruptedly the train of his thoughts. I therefore nodded in token of attention, and remained silent, although sadly tempted to ask a multiplicity of questions. After a pause of several minutes, which to me seemed like hours, Ibrahim was gracious enough to proceed, having in the mean time filled our glasses with the sparkling champagne that had been brought in by the beautiful Moorish girl.

"You tell me you have resolved," continued he, "to visit the Great Desert. As I regard you in the light of a friend, I wish to do you a service which may prove of great advantage to you.

"You are recommended by the French commander, and intend to travel in company with the French; but you would not be so secure among them as with the company in which I advise you to take this journey. The French are about to visit the Desert for the first time. Their intentions, they say, are friendly, and they claim to be actuated solely by the desire of subserving the cause of civilization, science, &c.,—as they call it; but the natives will decline to look upon the members of the expedition in any light but that of invaders. If you travel in their company without any other safeguard than the protection of the commander, you will expose yourself to dangers of the most formidable nature, springing from quarters whence they

are least expected. I have brought you here to make
you acquainted with one of the most powerful chiefs
of the Desert, the *Taleb* of Gherdaia,—a man who is
under many obligations to me, and to whom I have
rendered daily services for many years, for which, however, I desire no reward. But one favor I am about
to ask of him: I intend to intrust you to his care,
charging him with your safety, and requesting him to
bring you back to me should you decide to return by
this route on your way home from the Sahara."

These words of my friend deeply affected me. A
father could not have shown a deeper interest in my
welfare than that displayed by this man to whom one
month before I had been an utter stranger; and as I
thanked him in few but heartfelt words, and warmly
grasped his hand, my features must have fully spoken
the gratitude my tongue was unable to express.

In the course of the conversation that ensued, I was
made acquainted with the following facts.

About a year before Abd-el-Kader was taken prisoner by the French, Mussa-el-Darkui, a powerful
chief of the Sahara, had come from his sandy home
with a large force of horsemen, proclaiming to the
Arabs that he had been called by Allah to wage war
by fire and sword against the infidel, sparing none, and
that his mission was above all to punish the recreant
son of Mahiddin, Abd-el-Kader, who he asserted was
at that moment an ally of the French.

This fanatical Desert chief was not without a numerous following; for all the unscrupulous adventurers
who look to plunder above every thing else, and who,
of course, abound in a country like Algeria, flocked to
his standard.

At the tidings of Mussa's approach the Emir advanced to the Chelif, and reduced to subjection the powerful tribe of the Flitas, but did not venture to cross the river, which was the acknowledged boundary of his territory. Not long afterwards, however, he heard that Mussa-el-Darkui had made a triumphal entry into Medeah; whereupon, the imminence of the danger overcoming all prudential considerations, he crossed the Chelif and occupied Milianah, where the late Aga of the French, El-Hagi-Mahiddin-ben-Mubarek, and Mohammed-el-Barkani, former Kaid of Cherchell, entered his service.

At the hamlet of Amura, in the territory of the Summata, the hostile forces met. The Bedouins were commanded by the son of Mussa, the man in whose company I was to visit the Sahara. For a long time the contest was waged without any decisive results, the horsemen of the Emir and the wild sons of the Sahara manœuvring around each other for hours, yelling all the while like furious beasts of prey, but without coming to close quarters.

Abd-el-Kader's infantry force, however, was much more powerful than that of his opponent; and this fact, with the advantage given him by the possession of some cannon he had obtained from the French, at last decided the victory in his favor. The sunburnt children of the Sahara, who had never till then witnessed the destructive effects of artillery, broke in confusion before the murderous fire of the guns, and could not be induced to rally. Mussa, the chief, in company with a few trusty followers, fled to his home, hotly pursued by the horsemen of Abd-el-Kader. The power of the invaders was completely broken; and they never again ventured to attack the Emir or dispute his authority.

The wives and baggage of Mussa fell into the hands of the victor; but the Emir treated the women with the respect of a truly brave man, and generously sent them back to his defeated enemy, reserving only two out of the whole number,—one a girl of twelve, the youngest child of Mussa and the sister of the present chief of the Mozabites, the other a slave of rare beauty, whom Mussa had bought in Morocco for a fabulous price but a short time before he undertook his disastrous expedition against Abd-el-Kader.

These two girls were kept by the Emir as hostages until he was taken captive by the French. They were then delivered to a distant relative,—at the suggestion, it is asserted by some, of the French themselves, as a measure of policy to prevent Mussa from waging war against the new rulers of the Emir's dominions.

Ibrahim was appointed keeper of the two hostages, with the mutual consent of the French and of Abd-el-Kader; and for their benefit, as well as in the hope that his master might some day return from his captivity, he built the gem of a palace in which we were then seated, and which was at that very moment the abode of the daughter of Mussa-el-Darkui, the once formidable chieftain of the Mozabites.

A short sketch of the Mozabites, who inhabit the three largest oases of the Sahara, may not be out of place here.

The Beni-Mozab—otherwise called the Mozabites—are the original inhabitants of the oases. Some of them have settled in Algiers, and they are also found scattered throughout the province; but the difference be-

tween those who live in the cities and the untrammelled
sons of the Desert is as marked as that which exists
between the Chinese and the Japanese.

Very little is known of their former history. According to their oral traditions, their ancestors did not
always inhabit the Great Desert, but came from a
mountainous region in some remote quarter of the East,
whose shores were washed by the ocean. The Jews of
Africa believe that the Mozabites are the lineal descendants of the Moabites of Scripture, the offspring
of Moab the son of Lot, and long the troublesome
neighbors of the children of Israel. Their language is
entirely different from that of the Kabyls; though a
student would have no difficulty in tracing an affinity
between the two tongues.

During the time of the Helesen monarchy the tribe
of Moab was constantly persecuted; and this may serve
to explain their emigration to Africa, if it really did
take place. A circumstance that seems to corroborate
the hypothesis of the Mozabites being their descendants
is that the Mozabites are forbidden to enter the Mohammedan mosques in Algeria, just as Moab, in conformity with the ancient Hebrew law, was excluded
from the community of the Lord. Their present title,
Beni-Mozab, is of Semitic origin; and such names as
Ben-Salef, Ben-Elam, Ben-Jacob, Ben-Saul, and Ben-
Isaac are by no means uncommon among them.

Considerable information respecting this race was
supplied by the verbal narration of a French renegade who resided in Algeria between 1830 and 1835,
and who, becoming thoroughly conversant with the
Mozabitish manners and mode of life, was enabled to
visit their home in the oases of the Sahara. No other

European, before or since, has enjoyed this privilege. The most important town of which they had entire control was Gherdaia. Their form of government is that of a federated republic; and they are ever ready to sacrifice life and property, if need be, in defence of their independence.

As I shall on a future occasion have more to say concerning the Mozabites, this short description must suffice to give the reader an idea of the character of the people in whose company I was about to visit the Sahara.

A short time before my visit to Tlemcen, negotiations had been entered into with a view to the restoration of the two hostages, in which Ibrahim had taken an active part. The result had been an agreement to restore the women to their relatives; and the son of Mussa-el-Darkui, the present Taleb of Gherdaia, had arrived with a numerous retinue to escort his sister and her companion to their desert-home.

They had already been in Tlemcen for several days, the guests of Ibrahim, who intended before their departure to give them a feast, to which the principal personages of the Mozabites, with all the aristocracy of Tlemcen, were to be invited.

The company was to assemble at one o'clock; but as Ibrahim wished to make me acquainted with the chief, and to place me under his charge during my proposed visit to the Sahara, he had taken me to the palace some hours beforehand, that I might have an opportunity of deciding whether to accompany the chief or go with the French expedition.

As the mysteries that had puzzled me so much were now explained, I was in no hurry to make up my mind. At the same time, however, I was very curious to know something of the people with whom I might soon be travelling in the Desert; and, signifying my desire to Ibrahim, he proceeded to gratify me.

Our horses having been led to the principal staircase, we mounted and started for the temporary *duar* of the Mozabites, which was situated in a grove lying west of Tlemcen.

As Ibrahim was well known to them, we were conducted, immediately upon our arrival, to the tent of the chief, which stood in the centre of the encampment, the other tents being ranged around it in a circle.

Enoch-ben-Mussa, the chief of the Mozabites, was as fine a specimen of manhood as I ever met during my travels in Africa. Of imposing figure and majestic carriage, he looked every inch the independent nomad chieftain.

Our arrival having been announced to him, he awaited us at the entrance of his tent; and as soon as we alighted he led us into the interior. After the usual Eastern introduction to the chief, we were presented to the others, some twenty in number; and it may not be out of place to describe here the ceremony of their *salaams*.

The Beni-Mozab are exceedingly punctilious in their reception of visitors; and there are some compliments which are seldom if ever omitted.

On entering, my friend uttered the usual " Salaam Aleycam" (" Peace be with you"), at the same time raising his right hand to his left breast; but in saluting the chief, who was of higher rank than any other of the inmates, he placed his middle finger first upon his lips and then upon his forehead.

The host replied, "Aleycam salaam" ("Peace be with you"); "rachmad Allah wah barrakaw" ("the mercy and blessing of God be upon you").

A pause ensued, during which the whole party appeared to be surveying the new-comers. The silence was soon broken, however, by the expression, "Kaif Kaifak?" ("How are you?") to which my friend answered, "El ham doo lillah!" ("Praise be to God!") Instead of this question, the "Taip een?" ("Is it well with you?") is often asked; to which the usual response is, "Allah yesellimak!" ("May God preserve you!")

The salutations completed, we were shown to a divan which was made from the baggage and covered with a rich carpet. Soon after, two menials brought in a tray, on which were small *fingans* shaped like egg-cups, and a vase containing hot coffee. A pipe was then presented to each of us, with the request, "To fuddal" ("Partake").

Before taking the pipe, Ibrahim again touched his lips and forehead with his finger. After a few whiffs, the host, addressing my friend, said, "Wahashtineh" ("You have deserted us"); to which he answered, "Allah la wahashminak!" ("May God never desert you!")

The dress of the Beni-Mozab, as I saw it, consisted of a pair of drawers extending below the knee, over which fell a long gown (zaboot) of coarse white woollen stuff, open from the neck to the waist, with very capacious sleeves. The drawers and gown were all of home manufacture. On their feet were red slippers; and on their closely-shaved heads they wore white skull-caps, their only protection from the rays of the sun.

The more affluent of the Mozabites wear coarse blue

linen shirts, and linen frocks of the same form, and over the cotton skull-cap a " tarboush," or cap of red cloth. Some have a fine white muslin turban twisted in horizontal folds around their caps, and encircle their gown at the waist with a woollen shawl. A long spear, a dagger fastened above the elbow, and a charm attached to a twisted leather thong or a blue silk cord, used to draw up their sleeves, and which, crossing between the shoulders, hangs under the left arm, completes their costume.

During this visit I had no opportunity of seeing their wives; but I ascertained afterwards that the dress of their women is by no means so fantastic as that of the ladies of Algiers or Morocco. They wear a long blanket twisted around the body in a very curious manner. Those who can afford it have linen gowns dyed of different colors, and a *melayah*, which when they go out they put on to screen their faces from the gaze of strangers. Custom and religion enforce on them certain personal ablutions, and hence they are cleaner than the majority of Arab women.

At the moment of our arrival, the tribe was about to partake of the mid-day meal; and, a cordial invitation being extended to us, we could not do otherwise than accept.

In a short time a servant appeared with a washing apparatus, that ablutions might be performed according to the Mohammedan custom; and, since it is sometimes good policy to do in Rome as the Romans do, I concluded to follow the example of the others, and to go through the entire ceremony as coolly as if I had never known any other procedure.

The washing apparatus consisted of a shallow pewter

basin with a broad rim and a stand for soap in the
centre. The vessel containing the water was quite
large, as the contents had to serve for the whole company. Sometimes a clean napkin is given to each person ; but the Arabs of inferior rank are not so prodigal,
generally making one suffice for all.

With one knee on the ground, the servant presented
the wash-basin first to the chief, then to me, then to
Ibrahim, and afterwards to the rest of the company,
the highest in rank being served first.

The basin having been placed before me, I held my
hands over it while the servant poured the water upon
them. The lower part of the basin was covered with a
sieve, through which the soiled water passed. Soap is
always used ; and it is customary to produce as much
lather on the hands as possible, while at intervals the
attendant pours clean water on them from the jug.

Thus, as the reader will perceive, the hands are never
brought in contact with the impure water, fresh water
being poured over them at least half a dozen times
during this quick but thorough ablution. The Arab's
hands are decidedly the cleanest part of his person ; for
he sometimes washes them half a dozen times a day,
while he does not touch his face with water more than
once in a month.

The hand-washing completed, the dinner was served
on a sort of tray of Arab manufacture. The first course
consisted of a famous *pièce de résistance*,—a fat lamb
roasted whole and stuffed with rice well seasoned and
mixed with raisins.

Each person was provided with a spoon to help
himself to the stuffing, but had no other instrument
than his fingers with which to tear the meat from the

bones. At first I felt very reluctant to tuck up my sleeves and thrust my fingers into the mass of skin, flesh, and fat lying in the dish before me; but it looked tempting, and, hunger prompting me, I soon followed the example of my companions and partook as heartily as if I had never known any other way of eating.

For the first time in my life I disposed of a meal without the aid of knife and fork; and although I have not a word to offer in defence of the custom, I must acknowledge that the force of example and the sharp pangs of hunger would soon reconcile the most fastidious to it. And even here the distinctions which exist in civilized society are not unknown; for among the Arabs, as among Europeans, he who has mingled in good society may be recognized at once by his manner of eating.

The Arab of high rank, while eating, uses the thumb and two fingers only, never reaching to the farther side of the dish, and taking but a small piece at a time. The vulgar Oriental, on the contrary, thrusts his whole hand into the dish, tears off huge pieces of the meat, smears himself with grease from ear to ear, and then caps the climax of ill manners by licking his fingers to clean them.

After the lamb came various stewed dishes, which, however, I found rather unpalatable, besides scalding my fingers in the attempt to partake of them. My friend Ibrahim laughed heartily at my discomfiture; but at last, with the assistance of a piece of bread, I managed to fish out a few of the morsels into which the meat was divided. As soon as these dishes were despatched, coffee and pipes were once more brought

in, and, the weighty business of eating being concluded, in a short time conversation became quite
animated.

Ibrahim now acquainted the party with my purpose
to visit the Sahara, and, in his desire to make an impression in my favor, gave a very strong coloring, to
say the least, to the truth. He told them that I would
greatly prefer their company on the journey to that of
the French, adding that I was not a Frenchman, and
was by no means partial to the French nation. Scarcely
had my friend uttered these words when the chief
sprang from his seat, and, advancing towards me,
grasped me warmly by both hands, exclaiming, " By
Allah, I will protect you as long as you are in the
Desert, and you shall be looked upon as one of ourselves." The manifest sincerity of this enthusiastic
outburst at once decided me to join them, and, having
announced my resolution, I was immediately made acquainted with the names and rank, in all their Eastern
wealth of detail, of the various personages with whom
I had just had the honor of dining.

As is the case with every one who has travelled extensively and lived among all sorts of people, it was
not long until I felt perfectly at home with my new
associates.

The salaam passed from mouth to mouth when I
pledged myself to go with them; while the chief seemed
overjoyed to have an opportunity of repaying in some
degree the kind offices of Ibrahim, who for six years
had been the faithful protector of his sister and her
companion.

The hour of the feast was now at hand; and, at my
friend's request, the chief, with the principal officers

of his retinue, prepared to set out for the palace. We were soon on the road, Ibrahim, the Beni-Mozab, and myself taking the lead on horseback, while the remainder of the party followed, some on dromedaries, others on camels.

As I had never yet been on the back of a dromedary, and as I was likely to find no other mode of conveyance in the Desert, the fancy seized me to make a beginning in that style of travel, and I requested one of the Mozabites to allow me to exchange animals with him. He readily agreed to do so; but I found my position on the dromedary's back an exceedingly awkward one, and the first movement of the animal convinced me that a horse, or even so ignoble a beast as the donkey, would be infinitely preferable as a means of locomotion.

A skilful rider on the dromedary retains his seat exclusively by preserving his balance. He crosses his legs in front, his right foot hanging over the left shoulder of the animal, and his left foot over the right shoulder; for stirrups cannot be used.

The only difference between the camel and the dromedary is that the latter is lighter, and therefore more gentle in its pace, than the former. The camel may be compared to the cart-horse; the dromedary, to the racer.

The animal I mounted certainly did not do discredit to the reputation of his species. Hardly had I got into position on his back, and crossed my legs in the most approved fashion, when off he started with a jump, and down I went, head over heels, sprawling on all-fours on the sand, and cutting a decidedly ridiculous figure.

Thus was I initiated into the mystery of dromedary-riding, paying for my first lesson with a somerset and exciting the hearty laughter of the entire cavalcade. I was urged to mount again, but declined, not knowing but that another attempt might eventuate in a broken limb, which would have been an unhappy augury of the result of my journey; and, besides, I was well aware that a sufficiency of practice was in store for me.

I soon effected a re-exchange of animals; and, as I galloped along on the noble charger of my friend Ibrahim, the dromedary did not stand high in my opinion as a means of conveyance. My mishap was the topic of conversation all along the road, the Mozabites being intensely amused at the result of my experiment.

We soon reached the mansion of my friend, where we found several guests from Tlemcen already arrived, and Madame Ibrahim doing the honors of the house in the absence of her husband. I was acquainted with nearly all present; for during my stay in the city I had mingled largely with the better class of society, foreign as well as native.

Most of the guests were sitting in the corridor; some were walking in the garden, while others were in the reception-room, admiring the paintings and other productions of European skill with which it was tastefully decorated.

At three o'clock precisely a signal was given by the discharge of a small cannon, and the French band, which had been brought from Tlemcen, played some beautiful airs. The musicians being concealed in a grove and the music heard from a distance, the effect was charming.

At four o'clock a sumptuous repast was served in a capacious tent which had been erected on the lawn.

I shall not attempt to specify the viands, but may remark that the whole affair was such as would have done honor to the most skilled of French cooks. I was a little anxious to see how the Mozabites would conduct themselves at table; and I found them quite as awkward in the use of knife and fork as I had been in dromedary-riding, which gave occasion for some good-humored raillery on my part in return for their laughter at my somerset.

Towards the close of the repast, and while the guests were still lingering at the table Madame Ibrahim requested me to take a seat by her side. I obeyed; whereupon, after a few minutes' desultory conversation, she told me she wished me to become particularly acquainted with two of my prospective fellow-travellers, and, taking my arm, she led me through the corridor into a small parlor, the door of which was opened by one of her maids, a sprightly Moorish girl.

This room I found in strict unison with the rest of the establishment, with but one exception : that whereas in all the other rooms of the palace that I had been permitted to enter I had beheld beautiful statues of marble, here the figures were alive. So unexpected was the vision that presented itself that I lacked the self-possession to advance, and remained as if spell-bound at the entrance.

On a gold-embroidered divan of blue velvet reclined a graceful figure, dressed after the fashion of Oriental women, but in colors so surpassingly rich as to dazzle the eyes of the beholder. A beautiful face, whose pallor was heightened by contrast with the heavy ringlets of glossy raven-black hair that fell in profusion around it, crowned the fairy figure, whose *tout-ensemble* was more like that of a poet's dream than of a flesh-and-blood-woman. At her feet, on a richly-embroidered tabouret, reclined another statue-like figure, her head resting on the knee of her companion and the paleness of her face rendered all the more striking by the dark color of her dress; while the two women constituted, in their unaffected grace, a group worthy of immortalization in marble by the master hand of a Canova.

When Madame Ibrahim had approached them so as nearly to touch their dress with hers, then, and not till then, did they show any sign of being conscious of our presence. The one on the tabouret now rose and made place for the intruder, with the air, as it seemed to me, of a person who has been disturbed in a pleasant revery. " Je viens vous présenter votre compagnon de voyage, ma chère Debora," said my hostess, on which announcement the lady addressed raised her head and smiled,—the smile which imparts so angelic an expression to the face that has been spiritualized by grief, and heightens the beauty with which nature may have endowed it,—and Madame Ibrahim thereupon introduced her to me as Debora-bath-Mussa, the sister of Enoch-ben-Mussa, chief of the Mozabites.

As I gazed upon her countenance, I no longer wondered that the Emir had retained her as a hostage : her loveliness was such that I dare not attempt to describe it, but must leave the reader to picture it in his imagination.

No one could have been long in her presence without perceiving that a deep grief was gnawing at the heart of this angelic creature and manifesting itself in every line of her face. This beautiful child of the

Desert, of keenly susceptible disposition, as are all her sisters of the East, had for years been living among civilized people, in the enjoyment of every luxurious appliance that modern refinement has devised. She had become thoroughly accustomed to the habits and manner of life of her captors, and had almost entirely forgotten her native land. Surrounded by all that her heart could desire, the thought of her desert-home had seemed little else than a wild dream, the outlines of which had been almost completely effaced by the hand of Time. And now she was reclaimed by her people, and was doomed to return to the wild, nomadic life of the Sahara, where woman is looked upon merely as the slave of man, bound to minister to his every caprice, either as an overtasked drudge or as a gilded toy.

And yet, although accustomed to European life and manners, and having ripened into womanhood in the bosom of a society which regards the sexes as equal, the pride that is born with the Arab woman would not suffer her to betray, to the men who had come to claim her as their own, that her heart was with those who were strangers and enemies to her kindred. Not a murmur escaped her lips, not a sigh heaved her bosom : she suffered in uncomplaining silence; but it was impossible for her to conceal from an observant eye the traces of the fierce struggle that was being waged under that calm exterior, and the marble paleness of her face bespoke too plainly the worm that was gnawing within.

Zelma, the slave of Mussa, and the companion of Deborah, was also wondrously beautiful; but her beauty was of a very different stamp from that of her

mistress. She was such a woman as would be adored
by the majority of men for external loveliness alone;
such a one as we may suppose the mother of the human
race to have been ere the Creator endowed her with an
immortal soul.

In a few well-chosen words Deborah signified her
gratification at the prospect of having a European for
a fellow-traveller, and promised that, although she had
so long been absent from her childhood's home, she
would try to render my stay in the oasis as little
irksome to me as possible, if she failed to make it
altogether agreeable.

Madame Ibrahim now invited her to accompany us
to the feast; but she resolutely declined, although it
had been given in her honor, as an affectionate farewell
to the beauteous child of the Desert. Seeing that per-
suasions were fruitless, my friend at length desisted,
and we bade the lovely pair adieu.

I could thoroughly appreciate the poor girl's feelings. The presence at the feast of her beloved friends
from Tlemcen, from whom she was now about to part,
perhaps forever, contrasted with that of her Desert
kinsmen, with whom her lot was henceforth to be cast
in, could not fail to excite emotions which she dis-
trusted her ability to conceal, and which if betrayed
might be productive of the most unhappy consequences
in her after-life.

On our way back, we met several of her friends who
were going to the apartment we had just left, to take
leave of the beautiful Deborah, as she was called. All
regretted the necessity of her departure; but no one
ventured to persuade her to rebel against those who
had come to claim her.

Rejoining the guests, we found them getting ready to witness the Arab war-dance, which had been arranged as part of the programme for the festivities.

Outside of the garden was an extensive lawn; and on a slight elevation beyond it were arranged divans for the accommodation of the invited guests, who were now seating themselves, the band of the Zouaves, meanwhile, playing an Algerine march, which, it seemed to me, sounded better on the soil of Algeria than it could possibly have done anywhere else.

As the performers in the play which was to be enacted had not yet arrived, coffee and pipes were served to such of the guests as chose to adopt that method of whiling away the time. The ground on which the exhibition was to take place was public property, and hence could not be monopolized by the guests; and it seemed to me that the entire population of Tlemcen, old and young, men, women, and children, Arabs, Jews, Moors, Koloughs, and negroes, had assembled to witness the Arab war-dance.

Some thirty minutes had been occupied in coffee-drinking, smoking, and general conversation, when suddenly a martial bugle-blast was heard in the distance. To the European it sounded harsh and discordant; but to the natives it appeared to be welcome music, for no sooner had they heard it than they clapped their hands enthusiastically and answered with the war-cry of "Allah and Mohammed!"

In the direction from which the sound had proceeded, there now came in sight some two hundred Arab horsemen, dashing along on their fiery steeds, whose hoofs seemed scarcely to touch the ground. On they came, their white burnouses flashing in the rays of the setting sun, until they arrived in front of the divan where sat the French commandant of Tlemcen, the Cadi, and my friend Ibrahim. There they halted, and drew up in line. It was the first time I had ever seen so many Arab horsemen together; and the spectacle was to me an exceedingly imposing one. I was afterwards informed that these men were members of a tribe living about half-way between Oran and Tlemcen, and that every one of them had participated in various battles during the war waged against the French by Abd-el-Kader: so that what they were now about to rehearse as an entertainment for our company was the counterpart of what had but a few years before been stern reality; and doubtless there were many in that line of half-savage horsemen whose proudest boast was of the number of Christians they had slain in deadly combat.

After the military salute to the French and Arab authorities, the leader rode forward and received from the hands of Ibrahim a rich flag emblazoned with the crescent, purporting to be a gift to the tribe from their beloved chief the Emir, now a captive in France.

Immediately thereafter the equestrian evolutions began. I have had the opportunity, during my travels, of judging of the proficiency of the various arms of the military service in almost every nation of Europe; and I believe I do not exaggerate when I say that nowhere have I seen infantry—to say nothing of cavalry—move with greater precision than did those wild Arab horsemen. Their movements were so rapidly executed, so manifold, and so exact that it was sometimes difficult to realize that the whole troop was not one solid mass, pervaded by a single will.

After these evolutions, which were executed *en masse*, in *carré*, in circle, and in four divisions, the notes of the bugle once more rang out, upon which the horsemen formed into groups of five, placing themselves at considerable intervals, and then, at a given signal, rushed towards each other with such fury that it seemed to me some broken limbs and fractured skulls would inevitably result. However, my fears proved groundless; and the troop soon reformed, in readiness for other evolutions.

The most exciting of all was what the Arabs called the "raka faka." They formed a square, of fifty horsemen to a side, placed at intervals of about ten yards. At the word of command, those on the sides galloped towards the places occupied by the men on the front and the rear, and *vice versa*, at the same time throwing their lances with what seemed to me a frightful disregard of consequences. Here and there in the apparently confused mass would every now and then be seen a rider hotly pressed, who would disappear under his horse as if overwhelmed, but only to reappear the next moment on the other side and assume the offensive.

The agility of the Arab horseman is equalled only by that of the Indian of the far West or of the Gaucho of the South American Pampas. He twines himself like a serpent around his horse while the animal is in full career; he sits, reclines, stands up on him, without either saddle or bridle, the mane of the horse being his only hold.

Another of their performances was as follows. The members of the troop dispersed to various distances, observing no fixed order, but keeping up a constant

discharge of their long carbines,—some firing over
their heads, others backward, and still others, apparently fastened under their horses, firing from between
the forelegs of the animals,—all this, be it remem-
bered, at full gallop.   At every new feat a wild shout
of applause rose from the spectators, the Europeans no
less than the native-born seeming to be enraptured with
the display.

The most brilliant feat of all was reserved for the
last.   In the centre of the lawn a circular space had
been marked out, in which a number of holes were
dug, wherein were deposited small bundles of various
descriptions of fireworks, all connected by one fuse so
as to admit of being discharged simultaneously.   On
and within this circle the Arabs now simulated a
bivouac.   All were clustered together in the various
postures of sleep, as if in camp for the night, when
suddenly the fuse was lighted and almost instanta-
neously the fireworks were ignited in the midst of the
apparently slumbering host.   As it was now quite
dark, the effect was superb.   One might easily have
imagined that the awakening men and horses were
standing on the brink of a volcano in eruption, enveloped as they seemed to be in fiery coruscations, and
with myriads of rockets rising from their midst.   Here
and there a bengalic fire threw its intense colored light
on the party, bringing out in strong relief the diverse
figures,—of whom some were grasping the manes of
their horses, as though just aroused from slumber,
others were running alongside of their animals, and
still others had mounted, displaying a skill in equestrianism that might have excited the envy of a circus-
rider,—but neither man nor beast passing for an instant

beyond the bounds of the prescribed circle. Amid the detonations of the fireworks, the shouts of the Arabs, the enthusiastic applause of the multitude, and the deafening uproar of the mob of urchins, this wild display terminated,—the most picturesque tableau it has ever been my fortune to witness.

The guests now returned to the interior of the palace-gardens, where the French band was still discoursing melodious sounds. The numerous kiosks, pagodas, and summer-houses were brilliantly illuminated with colored-paper lanterns of fantastic pattern, while the palace was one blaze of light from the wax tapers of the chandeliers that hung from the ceiling of the corridor.

During the evening I had a long conversation with Enoch-ben-Mussa about our intended journey, and was somewhat surprised to find that he meant to set out the next day but one. Still, as I had fully made up my mind to go, and as I required very little time for preparation, the shortness of the notice gave me no concern.

The next morning I was up betimes, and was soon busily engaged in purchasing the articles I was likely to find needful on my journey.

The prime necessity was a camel; and, as I wished to have one of my own, I decided to give my first attention to its purchase. Calling on a young Moor in Tlemcen whose acquaintance I had made during my stay in that city, I asked him to accompany me to one of the suburbs, where there was a large stall kept by an Arab camel-dealer; for I was well aware that a European is almost sure to be cheated if he undertakes to buy a camel without the aid of a con-

noisseur, especially if he is ignorant of the tricks of
the trade.

A Frenchman who had travelled for some time in
Algiers, making a collection of plants, told me that on
one occasion, while in an Arab village, he declared his
intention of buying a young camel, which he purposed
shipping to a friend, a large land-owner near Lyons.
No sooner had his desire become known in the place
than at least twenty camels were brought for his inspection. They were all fine-looking animals, in excellent condition, apparently: in fact, the only fault our
Frenchman could perceive was that they were too fat.
After a proper amount of deliberation and bargaining,
he selected the one which appeared to be the leanest,
and paid the price agreed upon. The next morning,
when he went to look at his fat camel, he found a
living skeleton, on whose almost fleshless bones the
skin hung in large folds, and whose best development
was about the joints. So marvellous a transformation
effected in a few hours rather mystified him, and he
called on the guide for an explanation, whereupon he
was told that it is the practice of many Arab camel-
dealers, when they desire to effect a sale, to make an
incision in the skin and inflate the animal until it looks
quite plump. It remains thus for a few hours, after
which it soon dwindles down to its original condition.
This trick is ordinarily practised with old animals;
and the metamorphosis is so complete that none but an
expert can detect it.

Armed with my knowledge of the Frenchman's experience, I went in company with my friend to make
my purchase. On arriving at the stall, we requested
to be shown some horses; but, after inspecting them

for a while, we pretended to have all at once changed our minds, and to have found out that what we really needed was a camel. By this means we threw them off their guard, and deprived them of the opportunity of fattening their camels. We selected a young and healthy beast, for which I had to pay a high price, but which nevertheless I considered a bargain.

Before we left the dealer's, I asked the Arab how they inflated the animals. He laughed; but, seeing that I knew something of the tricks of his brethren, and being moreover in high good humor at the thought of the sale he had just effected, he promised to elucidate the mystery.

From the very herd out of which I had selected my animal he took an old she-camel, a mass of skin and bones, and requested me to make a mark on its side with some red earth that he handed me, so that I could identify it again. This done, the camel was led away to the next stall, while my friend and I lighted pipes and were served with coffee. In less than twenty minutes the animal was brought in again, but so altered in appearance that I could not believe it was the same until I clearly distinguished the mark I had made, which, like the camel itself, had grown larger.

The Arab now let me into the secret of this mode of "raising the wind" in Africa. An incision about an inch in length is made in each ear, between the skin and the flesh. Into this a small tube is fitted, and secured by a strong silk cord. There it remains, hidden from the observation of all but the initiated, and ready for use at any moment.   .

When a merchant who is not acquainted with the blowing-up trick comes to buy a camel, the dealer

takes two tubes, each a yard long, and inserting one
end of each in the small tube which I have just described, through the other ends two Arabs blow with
all their might until the animal has attained the requisite degree of plumpness. The inflating tubes are
then withdrawn, and the air is prevented from escaping
by means of a small cork smeared with pitch.

The poor camel now becomes apparently quite lively
and frisky, trying to throw itself on the ground, or to
press against a wall, or a tree, or whatever other object
may be at hand, so as to get rid of the wind. It is
generally too well watched by the rascally Arab to
succeed in accomplishing its purpose. Sometimes, however, it manages to elude his vigilance; and then, if
the cork is not very securely fastened, the wind escapes
with a whistle like that of a steam-engine, and the fine-
looking beast suddenly collapses into the miserable object it really is. The inflation must cause great suffering to the unfortunate creature; for it is constantly
shivering, and seems unable to rest for a minute in
one spot; but this is attributed by a novice to a lively
disposition.

Congratulating myself on having escaped this vil-
lany, I led my purchase home, pressing it here and
there from time to time, however, being still a little
doubtful whether I might not have been imposed
upon despite all my caution, and not certain but that
the animal had been inflated in some way unknown
to me.

My next purchase was an entire suit of Arab clothes.
Then, having bought some indispensable articles of food,
an abundant supply of cigars, and a few cases of wine,
I packed up my worldly goods and had them taken to

the *duar* of the Mozabites, who intended to start the next morning before daybreak.

The afternoon and evening I passed in visiting the many friends I had made in Tlemcen, and at one o'clock in the morning I set out for the Mozabite camp. Arrived there, I found the whole camp wrapped in slumber, with the exception of the sentinel, who was stationed outside of the *duar*, and who accosted me with the "Kaif Kaifak?" ("How are you?") to which I replied, "El ham doo lillah!" ("Praise be to God!")

I had sent before me a young lad whom I had hired as a domestic, and who had served five years in the house of Madame L—— at Tlemcen, and had been recommended to me for faithfulness and honesty,—qualifications seldom met with in Arab servants. He spoke French and Arabic fluently, was an excellent tailor and cook, and, in fact, was exactly such an attendant as I should need on my journey in the desert.

When I arrived at the tent where I had deposited my goods the day before, I found my boy Youssouf engaged in arranging my baggage, placing things in such a way that they might easily be got at if needed.

At three o'clock the camp was all alive. The camels were packed, the tents were taken up, and every thing was put in marching-order.

By the dim light of the breaking day I could discern a litter placed near the tent of the chief of the tribe. This, I readily surmised, was destined for Deborah and her companion.

At four o'clock every thing was in readiness, and I was just about to mount my camel, when I saw approaching two persons who had become greatly endeared to me during my sojourn in Tlemcen,—Ibrahim and his beautiful wife. The face of the latter bore evident traces of weeping; for she had just taken leave of her friend Deborah, whom she loved with all the affection of a sister. As she bade me farewell, she earnestly charged me to stay for some time in the oasis, until her friend should have become somewhat reconciled to her new home. Then, wishing me a prosperous journey, she hastened from the spot, her husband, apparently as deeply affected as herself, following her.

The bugle sounds; the caravan is about to set out; and here, dear reader, I part from you for the present, thanking you for your patience and indulgence, and hoping on some future occasion to have your company in the Great Desert of Sahara.

INDEX.

249

THE END.

www.ingramcontent.com/pod-product-compliance
Lightning Source LLC
Chambersburg PA
CBHW030359270326
41926CB00009B/1186